Gustave Le Bon

The Crowd

Study of the Popular Mind

Copyright:
Title: The Crowd - Study of the Popular Mind
Author: Gustave Le Bon
Publisher: Pretorian Books, Ul. Hristo Samsarov 9, 9000 Varna
ISBN: 9783903352407
Date: 05.12.2019

PREFACE

The following work is devoted to an account of the characteristics of crowds.

The whole of the common characteristics with which heredity endows the individuals of a race constitute the genius of the race. When, however, a certain number of these individuals are gathered together in a crowd for purposes of action, observation proves that, from the mere fact of their being assembled, there result certain new psychological characteristics, which are added to the racial characteristics and differ from them at times to a very considerable degree.

Organised crowds have always played an important part in the life of peoples, but this part has never been of such moment as at present. The substitution of the unconscious action of crowds for the conscious activity of individuals is one of the principal characteristics of the present age.

I have endeavoured to examine the difficult problem presented by crowds in a purely scientific manner—that is, by making an effort to proceed with method, and without being influenced by opinions, theories, and doctrines. This, I believe, is the only mode of arriving at the discovery of some few particles of truth, especially when dealing, as is the case here, with a question that is the subject of impassioned controversy. A man of science bent on verifying a phenomenon is not called upon to concern himself with the interests his verifications may hurt. In a recent publication an eminent thinker, M. Goblet d'Alviela, made the remark that, belonging to none of the contemporary schools, I am occasionally found in opposition of sundry of the conclusions of all of them. I hope this new work will merit a similar observation. To belong to a school is necessarily to espouse its prejudices and preconceived opinions.

Still I should explain to the reader why he will find me draw conclusions from my investigations which it might be thought at first sight they do not bear; why, for instance, after noting the extreme mental inferiority of crowds, picked assemblies included, I yet affirm it would be dangerous to meddle with their organisation, notwithstanding this inferiority.

The reason is, that the most attentive observation of the facts of history has invariably demonstrated to me that social organisms being every whit as complicated as those of all beings, it is in no wise in our power to force them to undergo on a sudden far-reaching transformations. Nature has recourse at times to radical measures, but never after our fashion, which explains how it is that nothing is more fatal to a people than the mania for great reforms, however excellent these reforms may appear theoretically. They would only be useful were it possible to change instantaneously the genius of nations. This power, however, is only possessed by time. Men are ruled by ideas, sentiments, and customs—matters which are of the essence of ourselves. Institutions and laws are the outward manifestation of our character, the expression of its needs. Being its outcome, institutions and laws cannot change this character.

The study of social phenomena cannot be separated from that of the peoples among whom they have come into existence. From the philosophic point of view these phenomena may have an absolute value; in practice they have only a relative value.

It is necessary, in consequence, when studying a social phenomenon, to consider it successively under two very different aspects. It will then be seen that the teachings of pure reason are very often contrary to those of practical reason. There are scarcely any data, even physical, to which this distinction is not applicable. From the point of view of absolute truth a cube or a circle are invariable geometrical figures, rigorously defined by certain formulas. From the point of view of the impression they make on our eye these geometrical figures may assume very varied shapes. By perspective the cube may be transformed into a pyramid or a square, the circle into an ellipse or a straight line. Moreover, the consideration of these fictitious shapes is far more important than that of the real shapes, for it is they and they alone that we see and that can be reproduced by photography or in pictures. In certain cases there is more truth in the unreal than in the real. To present objects with their exact geometrical forms would be to distort nature and render it unrecognisable. If we imagine a world whose inhabitants could only copy or photograph objects, but were unable to touch them, it would be very difficult for such persons to attain to an exact idea of their form. Moreover, the knowledge of this form, accessible only to a small number of learned men, would present but a very minor interest.

The philosopher who studies social phenomena should bear in mind that side by side with their theoretical value they possess a practical value, and that this latter, so far as the evolution of civilisation is concerned, is alone of importance. The recognition of this fact should render him very circumspect with regard to the conclusions that logic would seem at first to enforce upon him.

There are other motives that dictate to him a like reserve. The complexity of social facts is such, that it is impossible to grasp them as a whole and to foresee the effects of their reciprocal influence. It seems, too, that behind the visible facts are hidden at times thousands of invisible causes. Visible social phenomena appear to be the result of an immense, unconscious working, that as a rule is beyond the reach of our analysis. Perceptible phenomena may be compared to the waves, which are the expression on the surface of the ocean of deep-lying disturbances of which we know nothing. So far as the majority of their acts are considered, crowds display a singularly inferior mentality; yet there are other acts in which they appear to be guided by those mysterious forces which the ancients denominated destiny, nature, or providence, which we call the voices of the dead, and whose power it is impossible to overlook, although we ignore their essence. It would seem, at times, as if there were latent forces in the inner being of nations which serve to guide them. What, for instance, can be more complicated, more logical, more marvellous than a language? Yet whence can this admirably organised production have arisen, except it be the outcome of the unconscious genius of crowds? The most learned academics, the most esteemed grammarians can do no more than note down the laws that govern languages; they would be utterly incapable of creating them. Even with respect to the ideas of great men are we certain that they are exclusively the offspring of their brains? No doubt such ideas are always created by solitary minds, but is it not the genius of crowds that has furnished the thousands of grains of dust forming the soil in which they have sprung up?

Crowds, doubtless, are always unconscious, but this very unconsciousness is perhaps one of the secrets of their strength. In the natural world beings exclusively governed by instinct accomplish acts whose marvellous complexity astounds us. Reason is an attribute of humanity of too recent date and still too imperfect to reveal to us the laws of the unconscious, and still more to take its place. The part played by the unconscious in all our acts is immense, and that played by reason very small. The unconscious acts like a force still unknown.

If we wish, then, to remain within the narrow but safe limits within which science can attain to knowledge, and not to wander in the domain of vague conjecture and vain hypothesis, all we must do is simply to take note of such phenomena as are accessible to us, and confine ourselves to their consideration. Every conclusion drawn from our observation is, as a rule, premature, for behind the phenomena which we see clearly are other phenomena that we see indistinctly, and perhaps behind these latter, yet others which we do not see at all.

INTRODUCTION. THE ERA OF CROWDS.

The evolution of the present age—The great changes in civilisation are the consequence of changes in National thought—Modern belief in the power of crowds—It transforms the traditional policy of the European states—How the rise of the popular classes comes about, and the manner in which they exercise their power—The necessary consequences of the power of the crowd—Crowds unable to play a part other than destructive—The dissolution of worn-out civilisations is the work of the crowd—General ignorance of the psychology of crowds— Importance of the study of crowds for legislators and statesmen.

The great upheavals which precede changes of civilisations such as the fall of the Roman Empire and the foundation of the Arabian Empire, seem at first sight determined more especially by political transformations, foreign invasion, or the overthrow of dynasties. But a more attentive study of these events shows that behind their apparent causes the real cause is generally seen to be a profound modification in the ideas of the peoples. The true historical upheavals are not those which astonish us by their grandeur and violence. The only important changes whence the renewal of civilisations results, affect ideas, conceptions, and beliefs. The memorable events of history are the visible effects of the invisible changes of human thought. The reason these great events are so rare is that there is nothing so stable in a race as the inherited groundwork of its thoughts.

The present epoch is one of these critical moments in which the thought of mankind is undergoing a process of transformation.

Two fundamental factors are at the base of this transformation. The first is the destruction of those religious, political, and social beliefs in which all the elements of our civilisation are rooted. The second is the creation of entirely new conditions of existence and thought as the result of modern scientific and industrial discoveries.

The ideas of the past, although half destroyed, being still very powerful, and the ideas which are to replace them being still in process of formation, the modern age represents a period of transition and anarchy.

It is not easy to say as yet what will one day be evolved from this necessarily somewhat chaotic period. What will be the fundamental ideas on which the societies that are to succeed our own will be built up? We do not at present know. Still it is already clear that on whatever lines the societies of the future are organised, they will have to count with a new power, with the last surviving sovereign force of modern times, the power of crowds. On the ruins of so many ideas formerly considered beyond discussion, and to-day decayed or decaying, of so many sources of authority that successive revolutions have destroyed, this power, which alone has arisen in their stead, seems soon destined to absorb the others. While all our ancient beliefs are tottering and disappearing, while the old pillars of society are giving way one by one, the power of the crowd is the only force that nothing menaces, and of which the prestige is continually on the increase. The age we are about to enter will in truth be the ERA OF CROWDS.

Scarcely a century ago the traditional policy of European states and the rivalries of sovereigns were the principal factors that shaped events. The opinion of the masses scarcely counted, and most frequently indeed did not count at all. To-day it is the traditions which used to obtain in politics, and the individual tendencies and rivalries of rulers which do not count; while, on the contrary, the voice of the masses has become preponderant. It is this voice that dictates their conduct to kings, whose endeavour is to take note of its utterances. The destinies of nations are elaborated at present in the heart of the masses, and no longer in the councils of princes.

The entry of the popular classes into political life—that is to say, in reality, their progressive transformation into governing classes—is one of the most striking characteristics of our epoch of transition. The introduction of universal suffrage, which exercised for a long time but little influence, is not, as might be thought, the distinguishing feature of this transference of political power. The progressive growth of the power of the masses took place at first by the propagation of certain ideas, which have slowly implanted themselves in men's minds, and afterwards by the gradual association of individuals bent on bringing about the realisation of theoretical conceptions. It is by association that crowds have come to procure ideas with respect to their interests which are very clearly defined if not particularly just, and have arrived at a consciousness of their strength. The masses are founding syndicates before which the authorities capitulate one after the other; they are also founding labour unions, which in spite of all economic laws tend to regulate the conditions of labour and wages. They return to assemblies in which the Government is vested, representatives utterly lacking initiative and independence, and reduced most often to nothing else than the spokesmen of the committees that have chosen them.

To-day the claims of the masses are becoming more and more sharply defined, and amount to nothing less than a determination to utterly destroy society as it now exists, with a view to making it hark back to that primitive communism which was the normal condition of all human groups before the dawn of civilisation. Limitations of the hours of labour, the nationalisation of mines, railways, factories, and the soil, the equal distribution of all products, the elimination of all the upper classes for the benefit of the popular classes, &c., such are these claims.

Little adapted to reasoning, crowds, on the contrary, are quick to act. As the result of their present organisation their strength has become immense. The dogmas whose birth we are witnessing will soon have the force of the old dogmas; that is to say, the tyrannical and sovereign force of being above discussion. The divine right of the masses is about to replace the divine right of kings.

The writers who enjoy the favour of our middle classes, those who best represent their rather narrow ideas, their somewhat prescribed views, their rather superficial scepticism, and their at times somewhat excessive egoism, display profound alarm at this new power which they see growing; and to combat the disorder in men's minds they are addressing despairing appeals to those moral forces of the Church for which they formerly professed so much disdain. They talk to us of the bankruptcy of science, go back in penitence to Rome, and remind us of the teachings of revealed truth. These new converts forget that it is too late. Had they been really touched by grace, a like operation could not have the same influence on minds less concerned with the preoccupations which beset these recent adherents to religion. The masses repudiate to-day the gods which their admonishers repudiated yesterday and helped to destroy. There is no power, Divine or human, that can oblige a stream to flow back to its source.

There has been no bankruptcy of science, and science has had no share in the present intellectual anarchy, nor in the making of the new power which is springing up in the midst of this anarchy. Science promised us truth, or at least a knowledge of such relations as our intelligence can seize: it never promised us peace or happiness. Sovereignly indifferent to our feelings, it is deaf to our lamentations. It is for us to endeavour to live with science, since nothing can bring back the illusions it has destroyed.

Universal symptoms, visible in all nations, show us the rapid growth of the power of crowds, and do not admit of our supposing that it is destined to cease growing at an early date. Whatever fate it may reserve for us, we shall have to submit to it. All reasoning against it is a mere vain war of words. Certainly it is possible that the advent to power of the masses marks one of the last stages of Western civilisation, a complete return to those periods of confused anarchy which seem always destined to precede the birth of every new society. But may this result be prevented?

Up to now these thoroughgoing destructions of a worn-out civilisation have constituted the most obvious task of the masses. It is not indeed to-day merely that this can be traced. History tells us, that from the moment when the moral forces on which a civilisation rested have lost their strength, its final dissolution is brought about by those unconscious and brutal crowds known, justifiably enough, as barbarians. Civilisations as yet have only been created and directed by a small intellectual aristocracy, never by crowds. Crowds are only powerful for destruction. Their rule is always tantamount to a barbarian phase. A civilisation involves fixed rules, discipline, a passing from the instinctive to the rational state, forethought for the future, an elevated degree of culture—all of them conditions that crowds, left to themselves, have invariably shown themselves incapable of realising. In consequence of the purely destructive nature of their power crowds act like those microbes which hasten the dissolution of enfeebled or dead bodies. When the structure of a civilisation is rotten, it is always the masses that bring about its downfall. It is at such a juncture that their chief mission is plainly visible, and that for a while the philosophy of number seems the only philosophy of history.

Is the same fate in store for our civilisation? There is ground to fear that this is the case, but we are not as yet in a position to be certain of it.

However this may be, we are bound to resign ourselves to the reign of the masses, since want of foresight has in succession overthrown all the barriers that might have kept the crowd in check.

We have a very slight knowledge of these crowds which are beginning to be the object of so much discussion. Professional students of psychology, having lived far from them, have always ignored them, and when, as of late, they have turned their attention in this direction it has only been to consider the crimes crowds are capable of committing. Without a doubt criminal crowds exist, but virtuous and heroic crowds, and crowds of many other kinds, are also to be met with. The crimes of crowds only constitute a particular phase of their psychology. The mental constitution of crowds is not to be learnt merely by a study of their crimes, any more than that of an individual by a mere description of his vices.

However, in point of fact, all the world's masters, all the founders of religions or empires, the apostles of all beliefs, eminent statesmen, and, in a more modest sphere, the mere chiefs of small groups of men have always been unconscious psychologists, possessed of an instinctive and often very sure knowledge of the character of crowds, and it is their accurate knowledge of this character that has enabled them to so easily establish their mastery. Napoleon had a marvellous insight into the psychology of the masses of the country over which he reigned, but he, at times, completely misunderstood the psychology of crowds belonging to other races; and it is because he thus misunderstood it that he engaged in Spain, and notably in Russia, in conflicts in which his power received blows which were destined within a brief space of time to ruin it. A knowledge of the psychology of crowds is to-day the last resource of the statesman who wishes not to govern them—that is becoming a very difficult matter—but at any rate not to be too much governed by them.

It is only by obtaining some sort of insight into the psychology of crowds that it can be understood how slight is the action upon them of laws and institutions, how powerless they are to hold any opinions other than those which are imposed upon them, and that it is not with rules based on theories of pure equity that they are to be led, but by seeking what produces an impression on them and what seduces them. For instance, should a legislator, wishing to impose a new tax, choose that which would be theoretically the most just? By no means. In practice the most unjust may be the best for the masses. Should it at the same time be the least obvious, and apparently the least burdensome, it will be the most easily tolerated. It is for this reason that an indirect tax, however exorbitant it be, will always be accepted by the crowd, because, being paid daily in fractions of a farthing on objects of consumption, it will not interfere with the habits of the crowd, and will pass unperceived. Replace it by a proportional tax on wages or income of any other kind, to be paid in a lump sum, and were this new imposition theoretically ten times less burdensome than the other, it would give rise to unanimous protest. This arises from the fact that a sum relatively high, which will appear immense, and will in consequence strike the imagination, has been substituted for the unperceived fractions of a farthing. The new tax would only appear light had it been saved farthing by farthing, but this economic proceeding involves an amount of foresight of which the masses are incapable.

The example which precedes is of the simplest. Its appositeness will be easily perceived. It did not escape the attention of such a psychologist as Napoleon, but our modern legislators, ignorant as they are of the characteristics of a crowd, are unable to appreciate it. Experience has not taught them as yet to a sufficient degree that men never shape their conduct upon the teaching of pure reason.

Many other practical applications might be made of the psychology of crowds. A knowledge of this science throws the most vivid light on a great number of historical and economic phenomena totally incomprehensible without it. I shall have occasion to show that the reason why the most remarkable of modern historians, Taine, has at times so imperfectly understood the events of the great French Revolution is, that it never occurred to him to study the genius of crowds. He took as his guide in the study of this complicated period the descriptive method resorted to by naturalists; but the moral forces are almost absent in the case of the phenomena which naturalists have to study. Yet it is precisely these forces that constitute the true mainsprings of history.

In consequence, merely looked at from its practical side, the study of the psychology of crowds deserved to be attempted. Were its interest that resulting from pure curiosity only, it would still merit attention. It is as interesting to decipher the motives of the actions of men as to determine the characteristics of a mineral or a plant. Our study of the genius of crowds can merely be a brief synthesis, a simple summary of our investigations. Nothing more must be demanded of it than a few suggestive views. Others will work the ground more thoroughly. To-day we only touch the surface of a still almost virgin soil.

BOOK I: THE MIND OF CROWDS

CHAPTER I:
GENERAL CHARACTERISTICS OF CROWDS - PSYCHOLOGICAL LAW OF THEIR MENTAL UNITY

What constitutes a crowd from the psychological point of view—A numerically strong agglomeration of individuals does not suffice to form a crowd—Special characteristics of psychological crowds—The turning in a fixed direction of the ideas and sentiments of individuals composing such a crowd, and the disappearance of their personality—The crowd is always dominated by considerations of which it is unconscious—The disappearance of brain activity and the predominance of medullar activity—The lowering of the intelligence and the complete transformation of the sentiments—The transformed sentiments may be better or worse than those of the individuals of which the crowd is composed—A crowd is as easily heroic as criminal.

In its ordinary sense the word "crowd" means a gathering of individuals of whatever nationality, profession, or sex, and whatever be the chances that have brought them together. From the psychological point of view the expression "crowd" assumes quite a different signification. Under certain given circumstances, and only under those circumstances, an agglomeration of men presents new characteristics very different from those of the individuals composing it. The sentiments and ideas of all the persons in the gathering take one and the same direction, and their conscious personality vanishes. A collective mind is formed, doubtless transitory, but presenting very clearly defined characteristics. The gathering has thus become what, in the absence of a better expression, I will call an organised crowd, or, if the term is considered preferable, a psychological crowd. It forms a single being, and is subjected to the LAW OF THE MENTAL UNITY OF CROWDS.

It is evident that it is not by the mere fact of a number of individuals finding themselves accidentally side by side that they acquire the character of an organised crowd. A thousand individuals accidentally gathered in a public place without any determined object in no way constitute a crowd from the psychological point of view. To acquire the special characteristics of such a crowd, the influence is necessary of certain predisposing causes of which we shall have to determine the nature.

The disappearance of conscious personality and the turning of feelings and thoughts in a definite direction, which are the primary characteristics of a crowd about to become organised, do not always involve the simultaneous presence of a number of individuals on one spot. Thousands of isolated individuals may acquire at certain moments, and under the influence of certain violent emotions—such, for example, as a great national event—the characteristics of a psychological crowd. It will be sufficient in that case that a mere chance should bring them together for their acts to at once assume the characteristics peculiar to the acts of a crowd. At certain moments half a dozen men might constitute a psychological crowd, which may not happen in the case of hundreds of men gathered together by accident. On the other hand, an entire nation, though there may be no visible agglomeration, may become a crowd under the action of certain influences.

A psychological crowd once constituted, it acquires certain provisional but determinable general characteristics. To these general characteristics there are adjoined particular characteristics which vary according to the elements of which the crowd is composed, and may modify its mental constitution. Psychological crowds, then, are susceptible of classification; and when we come to occupy ourselves with this matter, we shall see that a heterogeneous crowd—that is, a crowd composed of dissimilar elements—presents certain characteristics in common with homogeneous crowds—that is, with crowds composed of elements more or less akin (sects, castes, and classes)—and side by side with these common characteristics particularities which permit of the two kinds of crowds being differentiated.

But before occupying ourselves with the different categories of crowds, we must first of all examine the characteristics common to them all. We shall set to work like the naturalist, who begins by describing the general characteristics common to all the members of a family before concerning himself with the particular characteristics which allow the differentiation of the genera and species that the family includes.

It is not easy to describe the mind of crowds with exactness, because its organisation varies not only according to race and composition, but also according to the nature and intensity of the exciting causes to which crowds are subjected. The same difficulty, however, presents itself in the psychological study of an individual. It is only in novels that individuals are found to traverse their whole life with an unvarying character. It is only the uniformity of the environment that creates the apparent uniformity of characters. I have shown elsewhere that all mental constitutions contain possibilities of character which may be manifested in consequence of a sudden change of environment. This explains how it was that among the most savage members of the French Convention were to be found inoffensive citizens who, under ordinary circumstances, would have been peaceable notaries or virtuous magistrates. The storm past, they resumed their normal character of quiet, law-abiding citizens. Napoleon found amongst them his most docile servants.

It being impossible to study here all the successive degrees of organisation of crowds, we shall concern ourselves more especially with such crowds as have attained to the phase of complete organisation. In this way we shall see what crowds may become, but not what they invariably are. It is only in this advanced phase of organisation that certain new and special characteristics are superposed on the unvarying and dominant character of the race; then takes place that turning already alluded to of all the feelings and thoughts of the collectivity in an identical direction. It is only under such circumstances, too, that what I have called above the PSYCHOLOGICAL LAW OF THE MENTAL UNITY OF CROWDS comes into play.

Among the psychological characteristics of crowds there are some that they may present in common with isolated individuals, and others, on the contrary, which are absolutely peculiar to them and are only to be met with in collectivities. It is these special characteristics that we shall study, first of all, in order to show their importance.

The most striking peculiarity presented by a psychological crowd is the following: Whoever be the individuals that compose it, however like or unlike be their mode of life, their occupations, their character, or their intelligence, the fact that they have been transformed into a crowd puts them in possession of a sort of collective mind which makes them feel, think, and act in a manner quite different from that in which each individual of them would feel, think, and act were he in a state of isolation. There are certain ideas and feelings which do not come into being, or do not transform themselves into acts except in the case of individuals forming a crowd. The psychological crowd is a provisional being formed of heterogeneous elements, which for a moment are combined, exactly as the cells which constitute a living body form by their reunion a new being which displays characteristics very different from those possessed by each of the cells singly.

Contrary to an opinion which one is astonished to find coming from the pen of so acute a philosopher as Herbert Spencer, in the aggregate which constitutes a crowd there is in no sort a summing-up of or an average struck between its elements. What really takes place is a combination followed by the creation of new characteristics, just as in chemistry certain elements, when brought into contact—bases and acids, for example—combine to form a new body possessing properties quite different from those of the bodies that have served to form it.

It is easy to prove how much the individual forming part of a crowd differs from the isolated individual, but it is less easy to discover the causes of this difference.

To obtain at any rate a glimpse of them it is necessary in the first place to call to mind the truth established by modern psychology, that unconscious phenomena play an altogether preponderating part not only in organic life, but also in the operations of the intelligence. The conscious life of the mind is of small importance in comparison with its unconscious life. The most subtle analyst, the most acute observer, is scarcely successful in discovering more than a very small number of the unconscious motives that determine his conduct. Our conscious acts are the outcome of an unconscious substratum created in the mind in the main by hereditary influences. This substratum consists of the innumerable common characteristics handed down from generation to generation, which constitute the genius of a race. Behind the avowed causes of our acts there undoubtedly lie secret causes that we do not avow, but behind these secret causes there are many others more secret still which we ourselves ignore. The greater part of our daily actions are the result of hidden motives which escape our observation.

It is more especially with respect to those unconscious elements which constitute the genius of a race that all the individuals belonging to it resemble each other, while it is principally in respect to the conscious elements of their character—the fruit of education, and yet more of exceptional hereditary conditions—that they differ from each other. Men the most unlike in the matter of their intelligence possess instincts, passions, and feelings that are very similar. In the case of every thing that belongs to the realm of sentiment—religion, politics, morality, the affections and antipathies, &c.—the most eminent men seldom surpass the standard of the most ordinary individuals. From the intellectual point of view an abyss may exist between a great mathematician and his boot maker, but from the point of view of character the difference is most often slight or non-existent.

It is precisely these general qualities of character, governed by forces of which we are unconscious, and possessed by the majority of the normal individuals of a race in much the same degree—it is precisely these qualities, I say, that in crowds become common property. In the collective mind the intellectual aptitudes of the individuals, and in consequence their individuality, are weakened. The heterogeneous is swamped by the homogeneous, and the unconscious qualities obtain the upper hand.

This very fact that crowds possess in common ordinary qualities explains why they can never accomplish acts demanding a high degree of intelligence. The decisions affecting matters of general interest come to by an assembly of men of distinction, but specialists in different walks of life, are not sensibly superior to the decisions that would be adopted by a gathering of imbeciles. The truth is, they can only bring to bear in common on the work in hand those mediocre qualities which are the birthright of every average individual. In crowds it is stupidity and not mother-wit that is accumulated. It is not all the world, as is so often repeated, that has more wit than Voltaire, but assuredly Voltaire that has more wit than all the world, if by "all the world" crowds are to be understood.

If the individuals of a crowd confined themselves to putting in common the ordinary qualities of which each of them has his share, there would merely result the striking of an average, and not, as we have said is actually the case, the creation of new characteristics. How is it that these new characteristics are created? This is what we are now to investigate.

Different causes determine the appearance of these characteristics peculiar to crowds, and not possessed by isolated individuals. The first is that the individual forming part of a crowd acquires, solely from numerical considerations, a sentiment of invincible power which allows him to yield to instincts which, had he been alone, he would perforce have kept under restraint. He will be the less disposed to check himself from the consideration that, a crowd being anonymous, and in consequence irresponsible, the sentiment of responsibility which always controls individuals disappears entirely.

The second cause, which is contagion, also intervenes to determine the manifestation in crowds of their special characteristics, and at the same time the trend they are to take. Contagion is a phenomenon of which it is easy to establish the presence, but that it is not easy to explain. It must be classed among those phenomena of a hypnotic order, which we shall shortly study. In a crowd every sentiment and act is contagious, and contagious to such a degree that an individual readily sacrifices his personal interest to the collective interest. This is an aptitude very contrary to his nature, and of which a man is scarcely capable, except when he makes part of a crowd.

A third cause, and by far the most important, determines in the individuals of a crowd special characteristics which are quite contrary at times to those presented by the isolated individual. I allude to that suggestibility of which, moreover, the contagion mentioned above is neither more nor less than an effect.

To understand this phenomenon it is necessary to bear in mind certain recent physiological discoveries. We know to-day that by various processes an individual may be brought into such a condition that, having entirely lost his conscious personality, he obeys all the suggestions of the operator who has deprived him of it, and commits acts in utter contradiction with his character and habits. The most careful observations seem to prove that an individual immerged for some length of time in a crowd in action soon finds himself—either in consequence of the magnetic influence given out by the crowd, or from some other cause of which we are ignorant—in a special state, which much resembles the state of fascination in which the hypnotised individual finds himself in the hands of the hypnotiser. The activity of the brain being paralysed in the case of the hypnotised subject, the latter becomes the slave of all the unconscious activities of his spinal cord, which the hypnotiser directs at will. The conscious personality has entirely vanished; will and discernment are lost. All feelings and thoughts are bent in the direction determined by the hypnotiser.

Such also is approximately the state of the individual forming part of a psychological crowd. He is no longer conscious of his acts. In his case, as in the case of the hypnotised subject, at the same time that certain faculties are destroyed, others may be brought to a high degree of exaltation. Under the influence of a suggestion, he will undertake the accomplishment of certain acts with irresistible impetuosity. This impetuosity is the more irresistible in the case of crowds than in that of the hypnotised subject, from the fact that, the suggestion being the same for all the individuals of the crowd, it gains in strength by reciprocity. The individualities in the crowd who might possess a personality sufficiently strong to resist the suggestion are too few in number to struggle against the current. At the utmost, they may be able to attempt a diversion by means of different suggestions. It is in this way, for instance, that a happy expression, an image opportunely evoked, have occasionally deterred crowds from the most bloodthirsty acts.

We see, then, that the disappearance of the conscious personality, the predominance of the unconscious personality, the turning by means of suggestion and contagion of feelings and ideas in an identical direction, the tendency to immediately transform the suggested ideas into acts; these, we see, are the principal characteristics of the individual forming part of a crowd. He is no longer himself, but has become an automaton who has ceased to be guided by his will.

Moreover, by the mere fact that he forms part of an organised crowd, a man descends several rungs in the ladder of civilisation. Isolated, he may be a cultivated individual; in a crowd, he is a barbarian—that is, a creature acting by instinct. He possesses the spontaneity, the violence, the ferocity, and also the enthusiasm and heroism of primitive beings, whom he further tends to resemble by the facility with which he allows himself to be impressed by words and images—which would be entirely without action on each of the isolated individuals composing the crowd—and to be induced to commit acts contrary to his most obvious interests and his best-known habits. An individual in a crowd is a grain of sand amid other grains of sand, which the wind stirs up at will.

It is for these reasons that juries are seen to deliver verdicts of which each individual juror would disapprove, that parliamentary assemblies adopt laws and measures of which each of their members would disapprove in his own person. Taken separately, the men of the Convention were enlightened citizens of peaceful habits. United in a crowd, they did not hesitate to give their adhesion to the most savage proposals, to guillotine individuals most clearly innocent, and, contrary to their interests, to renounce their inviolability and to decimate themselves.

It is not only by his acts that the individual in a crowd differs essentially from himself. Even before he has entirely lost his independence, his ideas and feelings have undergone a transformation, and the transformation is so profound as to change the miser into a spendthrift, the sceptic into a believer, the honest man into a criminal, and the coward into a hero. The renunciation of all its privileges which the nobility voted in a moment of enthusiasm during the celebrated night of August 4, 1789, would certainly never have been consented to by any of its members taken singly.

The conclusion to be drawn from what precedes is, that the crowd is always intellectually inferior to the isolated individual, but that, from the point of view of feelings and of the acts these feelings provoke, the crowd may, according to circumstances, he better or worse than the individual. All depends on the nature of the suggestion to which the crowd is exposed. This is the point that has been completely misunderstood by writers who have only studied crowds from the criminal point of view. Doubtless a crowd is often criminal, but also it is often heroic. It is crowds rather than isolated individuals that may be induced to run the risk of death to secure the triumph of a creed or an idea, that may be fired with enthusiasm for glory and honour, that are led on—almost without bread and without arms, as in the age of the Crusades—to deliver the tomb of Christ from the infidel, or, as in '93, to defend the fatherland. Such heroism is without doubt somewhat unconscious, but it is of such heroism that history is made. Were peoples only to be credited with the great actions performed in cold blood, the annals of the world would register but few of them.

CHAPTER II: THE SENTIMENTS AND MORALITY OF CROWDS

1. IMPULSIVENESS, MOBILITY, AND IRRITABILITY OF CROWDS. The crowd is at the mercy of all exterior exciting causes, and reflects their incessant variations—The impulses which the crowd obeys are so imperious as to annihilate the feeling of personal interest— Premeditation is absent from crowds—Racial influence. 2. CROWDS ARE CREDULOUS AND READILY INFLUENCED BY SUGGESTION. The obedience of crowds to suggestions—The images evoked in the mind of crowds are accepted by them as realities—Why these images are identical for all the individuals composing a crowd—The equality of the educated and the ignorant man in a crowd—Various examples of the illusions to which the individuals in a crowd are subject—The impossibility of according belief to the testimony of crowds—The unanimity of numerous witnesses is one of the worst proofs that can be invoked to establish a fact—The slight value of works of history. 3. THE EXAGGERATION AND INGENUOUSNESS OF THE SENTIMENTS OF CROWDS. Crowds do not admit doubt or uncertainty, and always go to extremes—Their sentiments always excessive. 4. THE INTOLERANCE, DICTATORIALNESS, AND CONSERVATISM OF CROWDS. The reasons of these sentiments—The servility of crowds in the face of a strong authority—The momentary revolutionary instincts of crowds do not prevent them from being extremely conservative—Crowds instinctively hostile to changes and progress. 5. THE MORALITY OF CROWDS. The morality of crowds, according to the suggestions under which they act, may be much lower or much higher than that of the individuals composing them—Explanation and examples—Crowds rarely guided by those considerations of interest which are most often the exclusive motives of the isolated individual—The moralising role of crowds.

Having indicated in a general way the principal characteristics of crowds, it remains to study these characteristics in detail.

It will be remarked that among the special characteristics of crowds there are several—such as impulsiveness, irritability, incapacity to reason, the absence of judgment and of the critical spirit, the exaggeration of the sentiments, and others besides—which are almost always observed in beings belonging to inferior forms of evolution—in women, savages, and children, for instance. However, I merely indicate this analogy in passing; its demonstration is outside the scope of this work. It would, moreover, be useless for persons acquainted with the psychology of primitive beings, and would scarcely carry conviction to those in ignorance of this matter.

I now proceed to the successive consideration of the different characteristics that may be observed in the majority of crowds.

1. IMPULSIVENESS, MOBILITY, AND IRRITABILITY OF CROWDS

When studying the fundamental characteristics of a crowd we stated that it is guided almost exclusively by unconscious motives. Its acts are far more under the influence of the spinal cord than of the brain. In this respect a crowd is closely akin to quite primitive beings. The acts performed may be perfect so far as their execution is concerned, but as they are not directed by the brain, the individual conducts himself according as the exciting causes to which he is submitted may happen to decide. A crowd is at the mercy of all external exciting causes, and reflects their incessant variations. It is the slave of the impulses which it receives. The isolated individual may be submitted to the same exciting causes as the man in a crowd, but as his brain shows him the inadvisability of yielding to them, he refrains from yielding. This truth may be physiologically expressed by saying that the isolated individual possesses the capacity of dominating his reflex actions, while a crowd is devoid of this capacity.

The varying impulses to which crowds obey may be, according to their exciting causes, generous or cruel, heroic or cowardly, but they will always be so imperious that the interest of the individual, even the interest of self-preservation, will not dominate them. The exciting causes that may act on crowds being so varied, and crowds always obeying them, crowds are in consequence extremely mobile. This explains how it is that we see them pass in a moment from the most bloodthirsty ferocity to the most extreme generosity and heroism. A crowd may easily enact the part of an executioner, but not less easily that of a martyr. It is crowds that have furnished the torrents of blood requisite for the triumph of every belief. It is not necessary to go back to the heroic ages to see what crowds are capable of in this latter direction. They are never sparing of their life in an insurrection, and not long since a general, becoming suddenly popular, might easily have found a hundred thousand men ready to sacrifice their lives for his cause had he demanded it.

Any display of premeditation by crowds is in consequence out of the question. They may be animated in succession by the most contrary sentiments, but they will always be under the influence of the exciting causes of the moment. They are like the leaves which a tempest whirls up and scatters in every direction and then allows to fall. When studying later on certain revolutionary crowds we shall give some examples of the variability of their sentiments.

This mobility of crowds renders them very difficult to govern, especially when a measure of public authority has fallen into their hands. Did not the necessities of everyday life constitute a sort of invisible regulator of existence, it would scarcely be possible for democracies to last. Still, though the wishes of crowds are frenzied they are not durable. Crowds are as incapable of willing as of thinking for any length of time.

A crowd is not merely impulsive and mobile. Like a savage, it is not prepared to admit that anything can come between its desire and the realisation of its desire. It is the less capable of understanding such an intervention, in consequence of the feeling of irresistible power given it by its numerical strength. The notion of impossibility disappears for the individual in a crowd. An isolated individual knows well enough that alone he cannot set fire to a palace or loot a shop, and should he be tempted to do so, he will easily resist the temptation. Making part of a crowd, he is conscious of the power given him by number, and it is sufficient to suggest to him ideas of murder or pillage for him to yield immediately to temptation. An unexpected obstacle will be destroyed with frenzied rage. Did the human organism allow of the perpetuity of furious passion, it might be said that the normal condition of a crowd baulked in its wishes is just such a state of furious passion.

The fundamental characteristics of the race, which constitute the unvarying source from which all our sentiments spring, always exert an influence on the irritability of crowds, their impulsiveness and their mobility, as on all the popular sentiments we shall have to study. All crowds are doubtless always irritable and impulsive, but with great variations of degree. For instance, the difference between a Latin and an Anglo-Saxon crowd is striking. The most recent facts in French history throw a vivid light on this point. The mere publication, twenty-five years ago, of a telegram, relating an insult supposed to have been offered an ambassador, was sufficient to determine an explosion of fury, whence followed immediately a terrible war. Some years later the telegraphic announcement of an insignificant reverse at Langson provoked a fresh explosion which brought about the instantaneous overthrow of the government. At the same moment a much more serious reverse undergone by the English expedition to Khartoum produced only a slight emotion in England, and no ministry was overturned. Crowds are everywhere distinguished by feminine characteristics, but Latin crowds are the most feminine of all. Whoever trusts in them may rapidly attain a lofty destiny, but to do so is to be perpetually skirting the brink of a Tarpeian rock, with the certainty of one day being precipitated from it.

2. THE SUGGESTIBILITY AND CREDULITY OF CROWDS

When defining crowds, we said that one of their general characteristics was an excessive suggestibility, and we have shown to what an extent suggestions are contagious in every human agglomeration; a fact which explains the rapid turning of the sentiments of a crowd in a definite direction. However indifferent it may be supposed, a crowd, as a rule, is in a state of expectant attention, which renders suggestion easy. The first suggestion formulated which arises implants itself immediately by a process of contagion in the brains of all assembled, and the identical bent of the sentiments of the crowd is immediately an accomplished fact.

As is the case with all persons under the influence of suggestion, the idea which has entered the brain tends to transform itself into an act. Whether the act is that of setting fire to a palace, or involves self-sacrifice, a crowd lends itself to it with equal facility. All will depend on the nature of the exciting cause, and no longer, as in the case of the isolated individual, on the relations existing between the act suggested and the sum total of the reasons which may be urged against its realisation.

In consequence, a crowd perpetually hovering on the borderland of unconsciousness, readily yielding to all suggestions, having all the violence of feeling peculiar to beings who cannot appeal to the influence of reason, deprived of all critical faculty, cannot be otherwise than excessively credulous. The improbable does not exist for a crowd, and it is necessary to bear this circumstance well in mind to understand the facility with which are created and propagated the most improbable legends and stories.

The creation of the legends which so easily obtain circulation in crowds is not solely the consequence of their extreme credulity. It is also the result of the prodigious perversions that events undergo in the imagination of a throng. The simplest event that comes under the observation of a crowd is soon totally transformed. A crowd thinks in images, and the image itself immediately calls up a series of other images, having no logical connection with the first. We can easily conceive this state by thinking of the fantastic succession of ideas to which we are sometimes led by calling up in our minds any fact. Our reason shows us the incoherence there is in these images, but a crowd is almost blind to this truth, and confuses with the real event what the deforming action of its imagination has superimposed thereon. A crowd scarcely distinguishes between the subjective and the objective. It accepts as real the images evoked in its mind, though they most often have only a very distant relation with the observed fact.

The ways in which a crowd perverts any event of which it is a witness ought, it would seem, to be innumerable and unlike each other, since the individuals composing the gathering are of very different temperaments. But this is not the case. As the result of contagion the perversions are of the same kind, and take the same shape in the case of all the assembled individuals.

The first perversion of the truth effected by one of the individuals of the gathering is the starting-point of the contagious suggestion. Before St. George appeared on the walls of Jerusalem to all the Crusaders he was certainly perceived in the first instance by one of those present. By dint of suggestion and contagion the miracle signalised by a single person was immediately accepted by all.

Such is always the mechanism of the collective hallucinations so frequent in history—hallucinations which seem to have all the recognised characteristics of authenticity, since they are phenomena observed by thousands of persons.

To combat what precedes, the mental quality of the individuals composing a crowd must not be brought into consideration. This quality is without importance. From the moment that they form part of a crowd the learned man and the ignoramus are equally incapable of observation.

This thesis may seem paradoxical. To demonstrate it beyond doubt it would be necessary to investigate a great number of historical facts, and several volumes would be insufficient for the purpose.

Still, as I do not wish to leave the reader under the impression of unproved assertions, I shall give him some examples taken at hazard from the immense number of those that might be quoted.

The following fact is one of the most typical, because chosen from among collective hallucinations of which a crowd is the victim, in which are to be found individuals of every kind, from the most ignorant to the most highly educated. It is related incidentally by Julian Felix, a naval lieutenant, in his book on "Sea Currents," and has been previously cited by the Revue Scientifique.

The frigate, the Belle Poule, was cruising in the open sea for the purpose of finding the cruiser Le Berceau, from which she had been separated by a violent storm. It was broad daylight and in full sunshine. Suddenly the watch signalled a disabled vessel; the crew looked in the direction signalled, and every one, officers and sailors, clearly perceived a raft covered with men towed by boats which were displaying signals of distress. Yet this was nothing more than a collective hallucination. Admiral Desfosses lowered a boat to go to the rescue of the wrecked sailors. On nearing the object sighted, the sailors and officers on board the boat saw "masses of men in motion, stretching out their hands, and heard the dull and confused noise of a great number of voices." When the object was reached those in the boat found themselves simply and solely in the presence of a few branches of trees covered with leaves that had been swept out from the neighbouring coast. Before evidence so palpable the hallucination vanished.

The mechanism of a collective hallucination of the kind we have explained is clearly seen at work in this example. On the one hand we have a crowd in a state of expectant attention, on the other a suggestion made by the watch signalling a disabled vessel at sea, a suggestion which, by a process of contagion, was accepted by all those present, both officers and sailors.

It is not necessary that a crowd should be numerous for the faculty of seeing what is taking place before its eyes to be destroyed and for the real facts to be replaced by hallucinations unrelated to them. As soon as a few individuals are gathered together they constitute a crowd, and, though they should be distinguished men of learning, they assume all the characteristics of crowds with regard to matters outside their speciality. The faculty of observation and the critical spirit possessed by each of them individually at once disappears. An ingenious psychologist, Mr. Davey, supplies us with a very curious example in point, recently cited in the Annales des Sciences Psychiques, and deserving of relation here. Mr. Davey, having convoked a gathering of distinguished observers, among them one of the most prominent of English scientific men, Mr. Wallace, executed in their presence, and after having allowed them to examine the objects and to place seals where they wished, all the regulation spiritualistic phenomena, the materialisation of spirits, writing on slates, &c. Having subsequently obtained from these distinguished observers written reports admitting that the phenomena observed could only have been obtained by supernatural means, he revealed to them that they were the result of very simple tricks. "The most astonishing feature of Monsieur Davey's investigation," writes the author of this account, "is not the marvellousness of the tricks themselves, but the extreme weakness of the reports made with respect to them by the noninitiated witnesses. It is clear, then," he says, "that witnesses even in number may give circumstantial relations which are completely erroneous, but whose result is THAT, IF THEIR DESCRIPTIONS ARE ACCEPTED AS EXACT, the phenomena they describe are inexplicable by trickery. The methods invented by Mr. Davey were so simple that one is astonished that he should have had the boldness to employ them; but he had such a power over the mind of the crowd that he could persuade it that it saw what it did not see." Here, as always, we have the power of the hypnotiser over the hypnotised. Moreover, when this power is seen in action on minds of a superior order and previously invited to be suspicious, it is understandable how easy it is to deceive ordinary crowds.

Analogous examples are innumerable. As I write these lines the papers are full of the story of two little girls found drowned in the Seine. These children, to begin with, were recognised in the most unmistakable manner by half a dozen witnesses. All the affirmations were in such entire concordance that no doubt remained in the mind of the juge d'instruction. He had the certificate of death drawn up, but just as the burial of the children was to have been proceeded with, a mere chance brought about the discovery that the supposed victims were alive, and had, moreover, but a remote resemblance to the drowned girls. As in several of the examples previously cited, the affirmation of the first witness, himself a victim of illusion, had sufficed to influence the other witnesses.

In parallel cases the starting-point of the suggestion is always the illusion produced in an individual by more or less vague reminiscences, contagion following as the result of the affirmation of this initial illusion. If the first observer be very impressionable, it will often be sufficient that the corpse he believes he recognises should present— apart from all real resemblance—some peculiarity, a scar, or some detail of toilet which may evoke the idea of another person. The idea evoked may then become the nucleus of a sort of crystallisation which invades the understanding and paralyses all critical faculty. What the observer then sees is no longer the object itself, but the image evoked in his mind. In this way are to be explained erroneous recognitions of the dead bodies of children by their own mother, as occurred in the following case, already old, but which has been recently recalled by the newspapers. In it are to be traced precisely the two kinds of suggestion of which I have just pointed out the mechanism.

"The child was recognised by another child, who was mistaken.

The series of unwarranted recognitions then began.

"An extraordinary thing occurred. The day after a schoolboy had recognised the corpse a woman exclaimed, `Good Heavens, it is my child!'

"She was taken up to the corpse; she examined the clothing, and noted a scar on the forehead. `It is certainly,' she said, `my son who disappeared last July. He has been stolen from me and murdered.'

"The woman was concierge in the Rue du Four; her name was Chavandret. Her brother-in-law was summoned, and when questioned he said, `That is the little Filibert.' Several persons living in the street recognised the child found at La Villette as Filibert Chavandret, among them being the boy's schoolmaster, who based his opinion on a medal worn by the lad.

"Nevertheless, the neighbours, the brother-in-law, the schoolmaster, and the mother were mistaken. Six weeks later the identity of the child was established. The boy, belonging to Bordeaux, had been murdered there and brought by a carrying company to Paris."

It will be remarked that these recognitions are most often made by women and children—that is to say, by precisely the most impressionable persons. They show us at the same time what is the worth in law courts of such witnesses. As far as children, more especially, are concerned, their statements ought never to be invoked. Magistrates are in the habit of repeating that children do not lie. Did they possess a psychological culture a little less rudimentary than is the case they would know that, on the contrary, children invariably lie; the lie is doubtless innocent, but it is none the less a lie. It would be better to decide the fate of an accused person by the toss of a coin than, as has been so often done, by the evidence of a child.

To return to the faculty of observation possessed by crowds, our conclusion is that their collective observations are as erroneous as possible, and that most often they merely represent the illusion of an individual who, by a process of contagion, has suggestioned his fellows. Facts proving that the most utter mistrust of the evidence of crowds is advisable might be multiplied to any extent. Thousands of men were present twenty-five years ago at the celebrated cavalry charge during the battle of Sedan, and yet it is impossible, in the face of the most contradictory ocular testimony, to decide by whom it was commanded. The English general, Lord Wolseley, has proved in a recent book that up to now the gravest errors of fact have been committed with regard to the most important incidents of the battle of Waterloo—facts that hundreds of witnesses had nevertheless attested.

Such facts show us what is the value of the testimony of crowds. Treatises on logic include the unanimity of numerous witnesses in the category of the strongest proofs that can be invoked in support of the exactness of a fact. Yet what we know of the psychology of crowds shows that treatises on logic need on this point to be rewritten. The events with regard to which there exists the most doubt are certainly those which have been observed by the greatest number of persons. To say that a fact has been simultaneously verified by thousands of witnesses is to say, as a rule, that the real fact is very different from the accepted account of it.

It clearly results from what precedes that works of history must be considered as works of pure imagination. They are fanciful accounts of ill-observed facts, accompanied by explanations the result of reflection. To write such books is the most absolute waste of time. Had not the past left us its literary, artistic, and monumental works, we should know absolutely nothing in reality with regard to bygone times. Are we in possession of a single word of truth concerning the lives of the great men who have played preponderating parts in the history of humanity—men such as Hercules, Buddha, or Mahomet? In all probability we are not. In point of fact, moreover, their real lives are of slight importance to us. Our interest is to know what our great men were as they are presented by popular legend. It is legendary heroes, and not for a moment real heroes, who have impressed the minds of crowds.

Unfortunately, legends—even although they have been definitely put on record by books—have in themselves no stability. The imagination of the crowd continually transforms them as the result of the lapse of time and especially in consequence of racial causes. There is a great gulf fixed between the sanguinary Jehovah of the Old Testament and the God of Love of Sainte Therese, and the Buddha worshipped in China has no traits in common with that venerated in India.

It is not even necessary that heroes should be separated from us by centuries for their legend to be transformed by the imagination of the crowd. The transformation occasionally takes place within a few years. In our own day we have seen the legend of one of the greatest heroes of history modified several times in less than fifty years. Under the Bourbons Napoleon became a sort of idyllic and liberal philanthropist, a friend of the humble who, according to the poets, was destined to be long remembered in the cottage. Thirty years afterwards this easy-going hero had become a sanguinary despot, who, after having usurped power and destroyed liberty, caused the slaughter of three million men solely to satisfy his ambition. At present we are witnessing a fresh transformation of the legend. When it has undergone the influence of some dozens of centuries the learned men of the future, face to face with these contradictory accounts, will perhaps doubt the very existence of the hero, as some of them now doubt that of Buddha, and will see in him nothing more than a solar myth or a development of the legend of Hercules. They will doubtless console themselves easily for this uncertainty, for, better initiated than we are to-day in the characteristics and psychology of crowds, they will know that history is scarcely capable of preserving the memory of anything except myths.

3. THE EXAGGERATION AND INGENUOUSNESS OF THE SENTIMENTS OF CROWDS

Whether the feelings exhibited by a crowd be good or bad, they present the double character of being very simple and very exaggerated. On this point, as on so many others, an individual in a crowd resembles primitive beings. Inaccessible to fine distinctions, he sees things as a whole, and is blind to their intermediate phases. The exaggeration of the sentiments of a crowd is heightened by the fact that any feeling when once it is exhibited communicating itself very quickly by a process of suggestion and contagion, the evident approbation of which it is the object considerably increases its force.

The simplicity and exaggeration of the sentiments of crowds have for result that a throng knows neither doubt nor uncertainty. Like women, it goes at once to extremes. A suspicion transforms itself as soon as announced into incontrovertible evidence. A commencement of antipathy or disapprobation, which in the case of an isolated individual would not gain strength, becomes at once furious hatred in the case of an individual in a crowd.

The violence of the feelings of crowds is also increased, especially in heterogeneous crowds, by the absence of all sense of responsibility. The certainty of impunity, a certainty the stronger as the crowd is more numerous, and the notion of a considerable momentary force due to number, make possible in the case of crowds sentiments and acts impossible for the isolated individual. In crowds the foolish, ignorant, and envious persons are freed from the sense of their insignificance and powerlessness, and are possessed instead by the notion of brutal and temporary but immense strength.

Unfortunately, this tendency of crowds towards exaggeration is often brought to bear upon bad sentiments. These sentiments are atavistic residuum of the instincts of the primitive man, which the fear of punishment obliges the isolated and responsible individual to curb. Thus it is that crowds are so easily led into the worst excesses.

Still this does not mean that crowds, skilfully influenced, are not capable of heroism and devotion and of evincing the loftiest virtues; they are even more capable of showing these qualities than the isolated individual. We shall soon have occasion to revert to this point when we come to study the morality of crowds.

Given to exaggeration in its feelings, a crowd is only impressed by excessive sentiments. An orator wishing to move a crowd must make an abusive use of violent affirmations. To exaggerate, to affirm, to resort to repetitions, and never to attempt to prove anything by reasoning are methods of argument well known to speakers at public meetings.

Moreover, a crowd exacts a like exaggeration in the sentiments of its heroes. Their apparent qualities and virtues must always be amplified. It has been justly remarked that on the stage a crowd demands from the hero of the piece a degree of courage, morality, and virtue that is never to be found in real life.

Quite rightly importance has been laid on the special standpoint from which matters are viewed in the theatre. Such a standpoint exists no doubt, but its rules for the most part have nothing to do with common sense and logic. The art of appealing to crowds is no doubt of an inferior order, but it demands quite special aptitudes. It is often impossible on reading plays to explain their success. Managers of theatres when accepting pieces are themselves, as a rule, very uncertain of their success, because to judge the matter it would be necessary that they should be able to transform themselves into a crowd.

"Charley's Aunt," refused at every theatre, and finally staged at the expense of a stockbroker, has had two hundred representations in France, and more than a thousand in London. Without the explanation given above of the impossibility for theatrical managers to mentally substitute themselves for a crowd, such mistakes in judgment on the part of competent individuals, who are most interested not to commit such grave blunders, would be inexplicable. This is a subject that I cannot deal with here, but it might worthily tempt the pen of a writer acquainted with theatrical matters, and at the same time a subtle psychologist—of such a writer, for instance, as M. Francisque Sarcey.

Here, once more, were we able to embark on more extensive explanations, we should show the preponderating influence of racial considerations. A play which provokes the enthusiasm of the crowd in one country has sometimes no success in another, or has only a partial and conventional success, because it does not put in operation influences capable of working on an altered public.

I need not add that the tendency to exaggeration in crowds is only present in the case of sentiments and not at all in the matter of intelligence. I have already shown that, by the mere fact that an individual forms part of a crowd, his intellectual standard is immediately and considerably lowered. A learned magistrate, M. Tarde, has also verified this fact in his researches on the crimes of crowds. It is only, then, with respect to sentiment that crowds can rise to a very high or, on the contrary, descend to a very low level.

4. THE INTOLERANCE, DICTATORIALNESS AND CONSERVATISM OF CROWDS

Crowds are only cognisant of simple and extreme sentiments; the opinions, ideas, and beliefs suggested to them are accepted or rejected as a whole, and considered as absolute truths or as not less absolute errors. This is always the case with beliefs induced by a process of suggestion instead of engendered by reasoning. Every one is aware of the intolerance that accompanies religious beliefs, and of the despotic empire they exercise on men's minds.

Being in doubt as to what constitutes truth or error, and having, on the other hand, a clear notion of its strength, a crowd is as disposed to give authoritative effect to its inspirations as it is intolerant. An individual may accept contradiction and discussion; a crowd will never do so. At public meetings the slightest contradiction on the part of an orator is immediately received with howls of fury and violent invective, soon followed by blows, and expulsion should the orator stick to his point. Without the restraining presence of the representatives of authority the contradictor, indeed, would often be done to death.

Dictatorialness and intolerance are common to all categories of crowds, but they are met with in a varying degree of intensity. Here, once more, reappears that fundamental notion of race which dominates all the feelings and all the thoughts of men. It is more especially in Latin crowds that authoritativeness and intolerance are found developed in the highest measure. In fact, their development is such in crowds of Latin origin that they have entirely destroyed that sentiment of the independence of the individual so powerful in the Anglo-Saxon. Latin crowds are only concerned with the collective independence of the sect to which they belong, and the characteristic feature of their conception of independence is the need they experience of bringing those who are in disagreement with themselves into immediate and violent subjection to their beliefs. Among the Latin races the Jacobins of every epoch, from those of the Inquisition downwards, have never been able to attain to a different conception of liberty.

Authoritativeness and intolerance are sentiments of which crowds have a very clear notion, which they easily conceive and which they entertain as readily as they put them in practice when once they are imposed upon them. Crowds exhibit a docile respect for force, and are but slightly impressed by kindness, which for them is scarcely other than a form of weakness. Their sympathies have never been bestowed on easy-going masters, but on tyrants who vigorously oppressed them. It is to these latter that they always erect the loftiest statues. It is true that they willingly trample on the despot whom they have stripped of his power, but it is because, having lost his strength, he has resumed his place among the feeble, who are to be despised because they are not to be feared. The type of hero dear to crowds will always have the semblance of a Caesar. His insignia attracts them, his authority overawes them, and his sword instils them with fear.

A crowd is always ready to revolt against a feeble, and to bow down servilely before a strong authority. Should the strength of an authority be intermittent, the crowd, always obedient to its extreme sentiments, passes alternately from anarchy to servitude, and from servitude to anarchy.

However, to believe in the predominance among crowds of revolutionary instincts would be to entirely misconstrue their psychology. It is merely their tendency to violence that deceives us on this point. Their rebellious and destructive outbursts are always very transitory. Crowds are too much governed by unconscious considerations, and too much subject in consequence to secular hereditary influences not to be extremely conservative. Abandoned to themselves, they soon weary of disorder, and instinctively turn to servitude. It was the proudest and most untractable of the Jacobins who acclaimed Bonaparte with greatest energy when he suppressed all liberty and made his hand of iron severely felt.

It is difficult to understand history, and popular revolutions in particular, if one does not take sufficiently into account the profoundly conservative instincts of crowds. They may be desirous, it is true, of changing the names of their institutions, and to obtain these changes they accomplish at times even violent revolutions, but the essence of these institutions is too much the expression of the hereditary needs of the race for them not invariably to abide by it. Their incessant mobility only exerts its influence on quite superficial matters. In fact they possess conservative instincts as indestructible as those of all primitive beings. Their fetish- like respect for all traditions is absolute; their unconscious horror of all novelty capable of changing the essential conditions of their existence is very deeply rooted. Had democracies possessed the power they wield to-day at the time of the invention of mechanical looms or of the introduction of steam-power and of railways, the realisation of these inventions would have been impossible, or would have been achieved at the cost of revolutions and repeated massacres. It is fortunate for the progress of civilisation that the power of crowds only began to exist when the great discoveries of science and industry had already been effected.

5. THE MORALITY OF CROWDS

Taking the word "morality" to mean constant respect for certain social conventions, and the permanent repression of selfish impulses, it is quite evident that crowds are too impulsive and too mobile to be moral. If, however, we include in the term morality the transitory display of certain qualities such as abnegation, self-sacrifice, disinterestedness, devotion, and the need of equity, we may say, on the contrary, that crowds may exhibit at times a very lofty morality.

The few psychologists who have studied crowds have only considered them from the point of view of their criminal acts, and noticing how frequent these acts are, they have come to the conclusion that the moral standard of crowds is very low.

Doubtless this is often the case; but why? Simply because our savage, destructive instincts are the inheritance left dormant in all of us from the primitive ages. In the life of the isolated individual it would be dangerous for him to gratify these instincts, while his absorption in an irresponsible crowd, in which in consequence he is assured of impunity, gives him entire liberty to follow them. Being unable, in the ordinary course of events, to exercise these destructive instincts on our fellow- men, we confine ourselves to exercising them on animals. The passion, so widespread, for the chase and the acts of ferocity of crowds proceed from one and the same source. A crowd which slowly slaughters a defenceless victim displays a very cowardly ferocity; but for the philosopher this ferocity is very closely related to that of the huntsmen who gather in dozens for the pleasure of taking part in the pursuit and killing of a luckless stag by their hounds.

A crowd may be guilty of murder, incendiarism, and every kind of crime, but it is also capable of very lofty acts of devotion, sacrifice, and disinterestedness, of acts much loftier indeed than those of which the isolated individual is capable. Appeals to sentiments of glory, honour, and patriotism are particularly likely to influence the individual forming part of a crowd, and often to the extent of obtaining from him the sacrifice of his life. History is rich in examples analogous to those furnished by the Crusaders and the volunteers of 1793. Collectivities alone are capable of great disinterestedness and great devotion. How numerous are the crowds that have heroically faced death for beliefs, ideas, and phrases that they scarcely understood! The crowds that go on strike do so far more in obedience to an order than to obtain an increase of the slender salary with which they make shift. Personal interest is very rarely a powerful motive force with crowds, while it is almost the exclusive motive of the conduct of the isolated individual. It is assuredly not self-interest that has guided crowds in so many wars, incomprehensible as a rule to their intelligence—wars in which they have allowed themselves to be massacred as easily as the larks hypnotised by the mirror of the hunter.

Even in the case of absolute scoundrels it often happens that the mere fact of their being in a crowd endows them for the moment with very strict principles of morality. Taine calls attention to the fact that the perpetrators of the September massacres deposited on the table of the committees the pocket-books and jewels they had found on their victims, and with which they could easily have been able to make away. The howling, swarming, ragged crowd which invaded the Tuileries during the revolution of 1848 did not lay hands on any of the objects that excited its astonishment, and one of which would have meant bread for many days.

This moralisation of the individual by the crowd is not certainly a constant rule, but it is a rule frequently observed. It is even observed in circumstances much less grave than those I have just cited. I have remarked that in the theatre a crowd exacts from the hero of the piece exaggerated virtues, and it is a commonplace observation that an assembly, even though composed of inferior elements, shows itself as a rule very prudish. The debauchee, the souteneur, the rough often break out into murmurs at a slightly risky scene or expression, though they be very harmless in comparison with their customary conversation.

If, then, crowds often abandon themselves to low instincts, they also set the example at times of acts of lofty morality. If disinterestedness, resignation, and absolute devotion to a real or chimerical ideal are moral virtues, it may be said that crowds often possess these virtues to a degree rarely attained by the wisest philosophers. Doubtless they practice them unconsciously, but that is of small import. We should not complain too much that crowds are more especially guided by unconscious considerations and are not given to reasoning. Had they, in certain cases, reasoned and consulted their immediate interests, it is possible that no civilisation would have grown up on our planet and humanity would have had no history.

CHAPTER III: THE IDEAS, REASONING POWER, AND IMAGINATION OF CROWDS

1. THE IDEAS OF CROWDS. Fundamental and accessory ideas—How contradictory ideas may exist simultaneously—The transformation that must be undergone by lofty ideas before they are accessible to crowds— The social influence of ideas is independent of the degree of truth they may contain. 2. THE REASONING POWER OF CROWDS. Crowds are not to be influenced by reasoning—The reasoning of crowds is always of a very inferior order—There is only the appearance of analogy or succession in the ideas they associate. 3. THE IMAGINATION OF CROWDS. Strength of the imagination of crowds—Crowds think in images, and these images succeed each other without any connecting link—Crowds are especially impressed by the marvellous—Legends and the marvellous are the real pillars of civilisation—The popular imagination has always been the basis of the power of statesmen—The manner in which facts capable of striking the imagination of crowds present themselves for observation.

1. THE IDEAS OF CROWDS

WHEN studying in a preceding work the part played by ideas in the evolution of nations, we showed that every civilisation is the outcome of a small number of fundamental ideas that are very rarely renewed. We showed how these ideas are implanted in the minds of crowds, with what difficulty the process is effected, and the power possessed by the ideas in question when once it has been accomplished. Finally we saw that great historical perturbations are the result, as a rule, of changes in these fundamental ideas.

Having treated this subject at sufficient length, I shall not return to it now, but shall confine myself to saying a few words on the subject of such ideas as are accessible to crowds, and of the forms under which they conceive them.

They may be divided into two classes. In one we shall place accidental and passing ideas created by the influences of the moment: infatuation for an individual or a doctrine, for instance. In the other will be classed the fundamental ideas, to which the environment, the laws of heredity and public opinion give a very great stability; such ideas are the religious beliefs of the past and the social and democratic ideas of to-day.

These fundamental ideas resemble the volume of the water of a stream slowly pursuing its course; the transitory ideas are like the small waves, for ever changing, which agitate its surface, and are more visible than the progress of the stream itself although without real importance.

At the present day the great fundamental ideas which were the mainstay of our fathers are tottering more and more. They have lost all solidity, and at the same time the institutions resting upon them are severely shaken. Every day there are formed a great many of those transitory minor ideas of which I have just been speaking; but very few of them to all appearance seem endowed with vitality and destined to acquire a preponderating influence.

Whatever be the ideas suggested to crowds they can only exercise effective influence on condition that they assume a very absolute, uncompromising, and simple shape. They present themselves then in the guise of images, and are only accessible to the masses under this form. These imagelike ideas are not connected by any logical bond of analogy or succession, and may take each other's place like the slides of a magic-lantern which the operator withdraws from the groove in which they were placed one above the other. This explains how it is that the most contradictory ideas may be seen to be simultaneously current in crowds. According to the chances of the moment, a crowd will come under the influence of one of the various ideas stored up in its understanding, and is capable, in consequence, of committing the most dissimilar acts. Its complete lack of the critical spirit does not allow of its perceiving these contradictions.

This phenomenon is not peculiar to crowds. It is to be observed in many isolated individuals, not only among primitive beings, but in the case of all those—the fervent sectaries of a religious faith, for instance—who by one side or another of their intelligence are akin to primitive beings. I have observed its presence to a curious extent in the case of educated Hindoos brought up at our European universities and having taken their degree. A number of Western ideas had been superposed on their unchangeable and fundamental hereditary or social ideas. According to the chances of the moment, the one or the other set of ideas showed themselves each with their special accompaniment of acts or utterances, the same individual presenting in this way the most flagrant contradictions. These contradictions are more apparent than real, for it is only hereditary ideas that have sufficient influence over the isolated individual to become motives of conduct. It is only when, as the result of the intermingling of different races, a man is placed between different hereditary tendencies that his acts from one moment to another may be really entirely contradictory. It would be useless to insist here on these phenomena, although their psychological importance is capital. I am of opinion that at least ten years of travel and observation would be necessary to arrive at a comprehension of them.

Ideas being only accessible to crowds after having assumed a very simple shape must often undergo the most thoroughgoing transformations to become popular. It is especially when we are dealing with somewhat lofty philosophic or scientific ideas that we see how far-reaching are the modifications they require in order to lower them to the level of the intelligence of crowds. These modifications are dependent on the nature of the crowds, or of the race to which the crowds belong, but their tendency is always belittling and in the direction of simplification. This explains the fact that, from the social point of view, there is in reality scarcely any such thing as a hierarchy of ideas—that is to say, as ideas of greater or less elevation. However great or true an idea may have been to begin with, it is deprived of almost all that which constituted its elevation and its greatness by the mere fact that it has come within the intellectual range of crowds and exerts an influence upon them.

Moreover, from the social point of view the hierarchical value of an idea, its intrinsic worth, is without importance. The necessary point to consider is the effects it produces. The Christian ideas of the Middle Ages, the democratic ideas of the last century, or the social ideas of to-day are assuredly not very elevated. Philosophically considered, they can only be regarded as somewhat sorry errors, and yet their power has been and will be immense, and they will count for a long time to come among the most essential factors that determine the conduct of States.

Even when an idea has undergone the transformations which render it accessible to crowds, it only exerts influence when, by various processes which we shall examine elsewhere, it has entered the domain of the unconscious, when indeed it has become a sentiment, for which much time is required.

For it must not be supposed that merely because the justness of an idea has been proved it can be productive of effective action even on cultivated minds. This fact may be quickly appreciated by noting how slight is the influence of the clearest demonstration on the majority of men. Evidence, if it be very plain, may be accepted by an educated person, but the convert will be quickly brought back by his unconscious self to his original conceptions. See him again after the lapse of a few days and he will put forward afresh his old arguments in exactly the same terms. He is in reality under the influence of anterior ideas, that have become sentiments, and it is such ideas alone that influence the more recondite motives of our acts and utterances. It cannot be otherwise in the case of crowds.

When by various processes an idea has ended by penetrating into the minds of crowds, it possesses an irresistible power, and brings about a series of effects, opposition to which is bootless. The philosophical ideas which resulted in the French Revolution took nearly a century to implant themselves in the mind of the crowd. Their irresistible force, when once they had taken root, is known. The striving of an entire nation towards the conquest of social equality, and the realisation of abstract rights and ideal liberties, caused the tottering of all thrones and profoundly disturbed the Western world. During twenty years the nations were engaged in internecine conflict, and Europe witnessed hecatombs that would have terrified Ghengis Khan and Tamerlane. The world had never seen on such a scale what may result from the promulgation of an idea.

A long time is necessary for ideas to establish themselves in the minds of crowds, but just as long a time is needed for them to be eradicated. For this reason crowds, as far as ideas are concerned, are always several generations behind learned men and philosophers. All statesmen are well aware to-day of the admixture of error contained in the fundamental ideas I referred to a short while back, but as the influence of these ideas is still very powerful they are obliged to govern in accordance with principles in the truth of which they have ceased to believe.

2. THE REASONING POWER OF CROWDS

It cannot absolutely be said that crowds do not reason and are not to be influenced by reasoning.

However, the arguments they employ and those which are capable of influencing them are, from a logical point of view, of such an inferior kind that it is only by way of analogy that they can be described as reasoning.

The inferior reasoning of crowds is based, just as is reasoning of a high order, on the association of ideas, but between the ideas associated by crowds there are only apparent bonds of analogy or succession. The mode of reasoning of crowds resembles that of the Esquimaux who, knowing from experience that ice, a transparent body, melts in the mouth, concludes that glass, also a transparent body, should also melt in the mouth; or that of the savage who imagines that by eating the heart of a courageous foe he acquires his bravery; or of the workman who, having been exploited by one employer of labour, immediately concludes that all employers exploit their men.

The characteristics of the reasoning of crowds are the association of dissimilar things possessing a merely apparent connection between each other, and the immediate generalisation of particular cases. It is arguments of this kind that are always presented to crowds by those who know how to manage them. They are the only arguments by which crowds are to be influenced. A chain of logical argumentation is totally incomprehensible to crowds, and for this reason it is permissible to say that they do not reason or that they reason falsely and are not to be influenced by reasoning. Astonishment is felt at times on reading certain speeches at their weakness, and yet they had an enormous influence on the crowds which listened to them, but it is forgotten that they were intended to persuade collectivities and not to be read by philosophers. An orator in intimate communication with a crowd can evoke images by which it will be seduced. If he is successful his object has been attained, and twenty volumes of harangues—always the outcome of reflection—are not worth the few phrases which appealed to the brains it was required to convince.

It would be superfluous to add that the powerlessness of crowds to reason aright prevents them displaying any trace of the critical spirit, prevents them, that is, from being capable of discerning truth from error, or of forming a precise judgment on any matter. Judgments accepted by crowds are merely judgments forced upon them and never judgments adopted after discussion. In regard to this matter the individuals who do not rise above the level of a crowd are numerous. The ease with which certain opinions obtain general acceptance results more especially from the impossibility experienced by the majority of men of forming an opinion peculiar to themselves and based on reasoning of their own.

3. THE IMAGINATION OF CROWDS

Just as is the case with respect to persons in whom the reasoning power is absent, the figurative imagination of crowds is very powerful, very active and very susceptible of being keenly impressed. The images evoked in their mind by a personage, an event, an accident, are almost as lifelike as the reality. Crowds are to some extent in the position of the sleeper whose reason, suspended for the time being, allows the arousing in his mind of images of extreme intensity which would quickly be dissipated could they be submitted to the action of reflection. Crowds, being incapable both of reflection and of reasoning, are devoid of the notion of improbability; and it is to be noted that in a general way it is the most improbable things that are the most striking.

This is why it happens that it is always the marvellous and legendary side of events that more specially strike crowds. When a civilisation is analysed it is seen that, in reality, it is the marvellous and the legendary that are its true supports. Appearances have always played a much more important part than reality in history, where the unreal is always of greater moment than the real.

Crowds being only capable of thinking in images are only to be impressed by images. It is only images that terrify or attract them and become motives of action.

For this reason theatrical representations, in which the image is shown in its most clearly visible shape, always have an enormous influence on crowds. Bread and spectacular shows constituted for the plebeians of ancient Rome the ideal of happiness, and they asked for nothing more. Throughout the successive ages this ideal has scarcely varied. Nothing has a greater effect on the imagination of crowds of every category than theatrical representations. The entire audience experiences at the same time the same emotions, and if these emotions are not at once transformed into acts, it is because the most unconscious spectator cannot ignore that he is the victim of illusions, and that he has laughed or wept over imaginary adventures. Sometimes, however, the sentiments suggested by the images are so strong that they tend, like habitual suggestions, to transform themselves into acts. The story has often been told of the manager of a popular theatre who, in consequence of his only playing sombre dramas, was obliged to have the actor who took the part of the traitor protected on his leaving the theatre, to defend him against the violence of the spectators, indignant at the crimes, imaginary though they were, which the traitor had committed. We have here, in my opinion, one of the most remarkable indications of the mental state of crowds, and especially of the facility with which they are suggestioned. The unreal has almost as much influence on them as the real. They have an evident tendency not to distinguish between the two.

The power of conquerors and the strength of States is based on the popular imagination. It is more particularly by working upon this imagination that crowds are led. All great historical facts, the rise of Buddhism, of Christianity, of Islamism, the Reformation, the French Revolution, and, in our own time, the threatening invasion of Socialism are the direct or indirect consequences of strong impressions produced on the imagination of the crowd.

Moreover, all the great statesmen of every age and every country, including the most absolute despots, have regarded the popular imagination as the basis of their power, and they have never attempted to govern in opposition to it "It was by becoming a Catholic," said Napoleon to the Council of State, "that I terminated the Vendeen war. By becoming a Mussulman that I obtained a footing in Egypt. By becoming an Ultramontane that I won over the Italian priests, and had I to govern a nation of Jews I would rebuild Solomon's temple." Never perhaps since Alexander and Caesar has any great man better understood how the imagination of the crowd should be impressed. His constant preoccupation was to strike it. He bore it in mind in his victories, in his harangues, in his speeches, in all his acts. On his deathbed it was still in his thoughts.

How is the imagination of crowds to be impressed? We shall soon see. Let us confine ourselves for the moment to saying that the feat is never to be achieved by attempting to work upon the intelligence or reasoning faculty, that is to say, by way of demonstration. It was not by means of cunning rhetoric that Antony succeeded in making the populace rise against the murderers of Caesar; it was by reading his will to the multitude and pointing to his corpse.

Whatever strikes the imagination of crowds presents itself under the shape of a startling and very clear image, freed from all accessory explanation, or merely having as accompaniment a few marvellous or mysterious facts: examples in point are a great victory, a great miracle, a great crime, or a great hope. Things must be laid before the crowd as a whole, and their genesis must never be indicated. A hundred petty crimes or petty accidents will not strike the imagination of crowds in the least, whereas a single great crime or a single great accident will profoundly impress them, even though the results be infinitely less disastrous than those of the hundred small accidents put together. The epidemic of influenza, which caused the death but a few years ago of five thousand persons in Paris alone, made very little impression on the popular imagination. The reason was that this veritable hecatomb was not embodied in any visible image, but was only learnt from statistical information furnished weekly. An accident which should have caused the death of only five hundred instead of five thousand persons, but on the same day and in public, as the outcome of an accident appealing strongly to the eye, by the fall, for instance, of the Eiffel Tower, would have produced, on the contrary, an immense impression on the imagination of the crowd. The probable loss of a transatlantic steamer that was supposed, in the absence of news, to have gone down in mid-ocean profoundly impressed the imagination of the crowd for a whole week. Yet official statistics show that 850 sailing vessels and 203 steamers were lost in the year 1894 alone. The crowd, however, was never for a moment concerned by these successive losses, much more important though they were as far as regards the destruction of life and property, than the loss of the Atlantic liner in question could possibly have been.

It is not, then, the facts in themselves that strike the popular imagination, but the way in which they take place and are brought under notice. It is necessary that by their condensation, if I may thus express myself, they should produce a startling image which fills and besets the mind. To know the art of impressing the imagination of crowds is to know at the same time the art of governing them.

CHAPTER IV A RELIGIOUS SHAPE ASSUMED BY ALL THE CONVICTIONS OF CROWDS

What is meant by the religious sentiment—It is independent of the worship of a divinity—Its characteristics—The strength of convictions assuming a religious shape—Various examples—Popular gods have never disappeared—New forms under which they are revived—Religious forms of atheism—Importance of these notions from the historical point of view— The Reformation, Saint Bartholomew, the Terror, and all analogous events are the result of the religious sentiments of crowds and not of the will of isolated individuals.

We have shown that crowds do not reason, that they accept or reject ideas as a whole, that they tolerate neither discussion nor contradiction, and that the suggestions brought to bear on them invade the entire field of their understanding and tend at once to transform themselves into acts. We have shown that crowds suitably influenced are ready to sacrifice themselves for the ideal with which they have been inspired. We have also seen that they only entertain violent and extreme sentiments, that in their case sympathy quickly becomes adoration, and antipathy almost as soon as it is aroused is transformed into hatred. These general indications furnish us already with a presentiment of the nature of the convictions of crowds.

When these convictions are closely examined, whether at epochs marked by fervent religious faith, or by great political upheavals such as those of the last century, it is apparent that they always assume a peculiar form which I cannot better define than by giving it the name of a religious sentiment.

This sentiment has very simple characteristics, such as worship of a being supposed superior, fear of the power with which the being is credited, blind submission to its commands, inability to discuss its dogmas, the desire to spread them, and a tendency to consider as enemies all by whom they are not accepted. Whether such a sentiment apply to an invisible God, to a wooden or stone idol, to a hero or to a political conception, provided that it presents the preceding characteristics, its essence always remains religious. The supernatural and the miraculous are found to be present to the same extent. Crowds unconsciously accord a mysterious power to the political formula or the victorious leader that for the moment arouses their enthusiasm.

A person is not religious solely when he worships a divinity, but when he puts all the resources of his mind, the complete submission of his will, and the whole-souled ardour of fanaticism at the service of a cause or an individual who becomes the goal and guide of his thoughts and actions.

Intolerance and fanaticism are the necessary accompaniments of the religious sentiment. They are inevitably displayed by those who believe themselves in the possession of the secret of earthly or eternal happiness. These two characteristics are to be found in all men grouped together when they are inspired by a conviction of any kind. The Jacobins of the Reign of Terror were at bottom as religious as the Catholics of the Inquisition, and their cruel ardour proceeded from the same source.

The convictions of crowds assume those characteristics of blind submission, fierce intolerance, and the need of violent propaganda which are inherent in the religious sentiment, and it is for this reason that it may be said that all their beliefs have a religious form. The hero acclaimed by a crowd is a veritable god for that crowd. Napoleon was such a god for fifteen years, and a divinity never had more fervent worshippers or sent men to their death with greater ease. The Christian and Pagan Gods never exercised a more absolute empire over the minds that had fallen under their sway.

All founders of religious or political creeds have established them solely because they were successful in inspiring crowds with those fanatical sentiments which have as result that men find their happiness in worship and obedience and are ready to lay down their lives for their idol. This has been the case at all epochs. Fustel de Coulanges, in his excellent work on Roman Gaul, justly remarks that the Roman Empire was in no wise maintained by force, but by the religious admiration it inspired. "It would be without a parallel in the history of the world," he observes rightly, "that a form of government held in popular detestation should have lasted for five centuries.... It would be inexplicable that the thirty legions of the Empire should have constrained a hundred million men to obedience." The reason of their obedience was that the Emperor, who personified the greatness of Rome, was worshipped like a divinity by unanimous consent. There were altars in honour of the Emperor in the smallest townships of his realm. "From one end of the Empire to the other a new religion was seen to arise in those days which had for its divinities the emperors themselves. Some years before the Christian era the whole of Gaul, represented by sixty cities, built in common a temple near the town of Lyons in honour of Augustus.... Its priests, elected by the united Gallic cities, were the principal personages in their country.... It is impossible to attribute all this to fear and servility. Whole nations are not servile, and especially for three centuries. It was not the courtiers who worshipped the prince, it was Rome, and it was not Rome merely, but it was Gaul, it was Spain, it was Greece and Asia."

To-day the majority of the great men who have swayed men's minds no longer have altars, but they have statues, or their portraits are in the hands of their admirers, and the cult of which they are the object is not notably different from that accorded to their predecessors. An understanding of the philosophy of history is only to be got by a thorough appreciation of this fundamental point of the psychology of crowds. The crowd demands a god before everything else.

It must not be supposed that these are the superstitions of a bygone age which reason has definitely banished. Sentiment has never been vanquished in its eternal conflict with reason. Crowds will hear no more of the words divinity and religion, in whose name they were so long enslaved; but they have never possessed so many fetishes as in the last hundred years, and the old divinities have never had so many statues and altars raised in their honour. Those who in recent years have studied the popular movement known under the name of Boulangism have been able to see with what ease the religious instincts of crowds are ready to revive. There was not a country inn that did not possess the hero's portrait. He was credited with the power of remedying all injustices and all evils, and thousands of men would have given their lives for him. Great might have been his place in history had his character been at all on a level with his legendary reputation.

It is thus a very useless commonplace to assert that a religion is necessary for the masses, because all political, divine, and social creeds only take root among them on the condition of always assuming the religious shape—a shape which obviates the danger of discussion. Were it possible to induce the masses to adopt atheism, this belief would exhibit all the intolerant ardour of a religious sentiment, and in its exterior forms would soon become a cult. The evolution of the small Positivist sect furnishes us a curious proof in point. What happened to the Nihilist whose story is related by that profound thinker Dostoiewsky has quickly happened to the Positivists. Illumined one day by the light of reason he broke the images of divinities and saints that adorned the altar of a chapel, extinguished the candles, and, without losing a moment, replaced the destroyed objects by the works of atheistic philosophers such as Buchner and Moleschott, after which he piously relighted the candles. The object of his religious beliefs had been transformed, but can it be truthfully said that his religious sentiments had changed?

Certain historical events—and they are precisely the most important—I again repeat, are not to be understood unless one has attained to an appreciation of the religious form which the convictions of crowds always assume in the long run. There are social phenomena that need to be studied far more from the point of view of the psychologist than from that of the naturalist. The great historian Taine has only studied the Revolution as a naturalist, and on this account the real genesis of events has often escaped him. He has perfectly observed the facts, but from want of having studied the psychology of crowds he has not always been able to trace their causes. The facts having appalled him by their bloodthirsty, anarchic, and ferocious side, he has scarcely seen in the heroes of the great drama anything more than a horde of epileptic savages abandoning themselves without restraint to their instincts. The violence of the Revolution, its massacres, its need of propaganda, its declarations of war upon all things, are only to be properly explained by reflecting that the Revolution was merely the establishment of a new religious belief in the mind of the masses. The Reformation, the massacre of Saint Bartholomew, the French religious wars, the Inquisition, the Reign of Terror are phenomena of an identical kind, brought about by crowds animated by those religious sentiments which necessarily lead those imbued with them to pitilessly extirpate by fire and sword whoever is opposed to the establishment of the new faith. The methods of the Inquisition are those of all whose convictions are genuine and sturdy. Their convictions would not deserve these epithets did they resort to other methods.

Upheavals analogous to those I have just cited are only possible when it is the soul of the masses that brings them about. The most absolute despots could not cause them. When historians tell us that the massacre of Saint Bartholomew was the work of a king, they show themselves as ignorant of the psychology of crowds as of that of sovereigns. Manifestations of this order can only proceed from the soul of crowds. The most absolute power of the most despotic monarch can scarcely do more than hasten or retard the moment of their apparition. The massacre of Saint Bartholomew or the religious wars were no more the work of kings than the Reign of Terror was the work of Robespierre, Danton, or Saint Just. At the bottom of such events is always to be found the working of the soul of the masses, and never the power of potentates.

BOOK II: THE OPINIONS AND BELIEFS OF CROWDS

CHAPTER I: REMOTE FACTORS OF THE OPINIONS AND BELIEFS OF CROWDS

Preparatory factors of the beliefs of crowds—The origin of the beliefs of crowds is the consequence of a preliminary process of elaboration— Study of the different factors of these beliefs. 1. RACE. The predominating influence it exercises—It represents the suggestions of ancestors. 2. TRADITIONS. They are the synthesis of the soul of the race—Social importance of traditions—How, after having been necessary they become harmful—Crowds are the most obstinate maintainers of traditional ideas. 3. TIME. It prepares in succession the establishment of beliefs and then their destruction. It is by the aid of this factor that order may proceed from chaos. 4. POLITICAL AND SOCIAL INSTITUTIONS. Erroneous idea of their part—Their influence extremely weak—They are effects, not causes—Nations are incapable of choosing what appear to them the best institutions—Institutions are labels which shelter the most dissimilar things under the same title— How institutions may come to be created—Certain institutions theoretically bad, such as centralisation obligatory for certain nations. 5. INSTITUTIONS AND EDUCATION. Falsity of prevalent ideas as to the influence of instruction on crowds— Statistical indications—Demoralising effect of Latin system of education—Part instruction might play—Examples furnished by various peoples.

Having studied the mental constitution of crowds and become acquainted with their modes of feeling, thinking, and reasoning, we shall now proceed to examine how their opinions and beliefs arise and become established.

The factors which determine these opinions and beliefs are of two kinds: remote factors and immediate factors.

The remote factors are those which render crowds capable of adopting certain convictions and absolutely refractory to the acceptance of others. These factors prepare the ground in which are suddenly seen to germinate certain new ideas whose force and consequences are a cause of astonishment, though they are only spontaneous in appearance. The outburst and putting in practice of certain ideas among crowds present at times a startling suddenness. This is only a superficial effect, behind which must be sought a preliminary and preparatory action of long duration.

The immediate factors are those which, coming on the top of this long, preparatory working, in whose absence they would remain without effect, serve as the source of active persuasion on crowds; that is, they are the factors which cause the idea to take shape and set it loose with all its consequences. The resolutions by which collectivities are suddenly carried away arise out of these immediate factors; it is due to them that a riot breaks out or a strike is decided upon, and to them that enormous majorities invest one man with power to overthrow a government.

The successive action of these two kinds of factors is to be traced in all great historical events. The French Revolution—to cite but one of the most striking of such events—had among its remote factors the writings of the philosophers, the exactions of the nobility, and the progress of scientific thought. The mind of the masses, thus prepared, was then easily roused by such immediate factors as the speeches of orators, and the resistance of the court party to insignificant reforms.

Among the remote factors there are some of a general nature, which are found to underlie all the beliefs and opinions of crowds. They are race, traditions, time, institutions, and education.

We now proceed to study the influence of these different factors.

1. RACE

This factor, race, must be placed in the first rank, for in itself it far surpasses in importance all the others. We have sufficiently studied it in another work; it is therefore needless to deal with it again. We showed, in a previous volume, what an historical race is, and how, its character once formed, it possesses, as the result of the laws of heredity such power that its beliefs, institutions, and arts—in a word, all the elements of its civilisation—are merely the outward expression of its genius. We showed that the power of the race is such that no element can pass from one people to another without undergoing the most profound transformations.

Environment, circumstances, and events represent the social suggestions of the moment. They may have a considerable influence, but this influence is always momentary if it be contrary to the suggestions of the race; that is, to those which are inherited by a nation from the entire series of its ancestors.

We shall have occasion in several of the chapters of this work to touch again upon racial influence, and to show that this influence is so great that it dominates the characteristics peculiar to the genius of crowds. It follows from this fact that the crowds of different countries offer very considerable differences of beliefs and conduct and are not to be influenced in the same manner.

2. TRADITIONS

Traditions represent the ideas, the needs, and the sentiments of the past. They are the synthesis of the race, and weigh upon us with immense force.

The biological sciences have been transformed since embryology has shown the immense influence of the past on the evolution of living beings; and the historical sciences will not undergo a less change when this conception has become more widespread. As yet it is not sufficiently general, and many statesmen are still no further advanced than the theorists of the last century, who believed that a society could break off with its past and be entirely recast on lines suggested solely by the light of reason.

A people is an organism created by the past, and, like every other organism, it can only be modified by slow hereditary accumulations.

It is tradition that guides men, and more especially so when they are in a crowd. The changes they can effect in their traditions with any ease, merely bear, as I have often repeated, upon names and outward forms.

This circumstance is not to be regretted. Neither a national genius nor civilisation would be possible without traditions. In consequence man's two great concerns since he has existed have been to create a network of traditions which he afterwards endeavours to destroy when their beneficial effects have worn themselves out. Civilisation is impossible without traditions, and progress impossible without the destruction of those traditions. The difficulty, and it is an immense difficulty, is to find a proper equilibrium between stability and variability. Should a people allow its customs to become too firmly rooted, it can no longer change, and becomes, like China, incapable of improvement. Violent revolutions are in this case of no avail; for what happens is that either the broken fragments of the chain are pieced together again and the past resumes its empire without change, or the fragments remain apart and decadence soon succeeds anarchy.

The ideal for a people is in consequence to preserve the institutions of the past, merely changing them insensibly and little by little. This ideal is difficult to realise. The Romans in ancient and the English in modern times are almost alone in having realised it.

It is precisely crowds that cling the most tenaciously to traditional ideas and oppose their being changed with the most obstinacy. This is notably the case with the category of crowds constituting castes. I have already insisted upon the conservative spirit of crowds, and shown that the most violent rebellions merely end in a changing of words and terms. At the end of the last century, in the presence of destroyed churches, of priests expelled the country or guillotined, it might have been thought that the old religious ideas had lost all their strength, and yet a few years had barely lapsed before the abolished system of public worship had to be re-established in deference to universal demands.

"What is everywhere seen with respect to the keeping of Sunday and attendance at the churches proves that the majority of Frenchmen desire to return to their old usages and that it is no longer opportune to resist this natural tendency.... The great majority of men stand in need of religion, public worship, and priests. IT IS AN ERROR OF SOME MODERN PHILOSOPHERS, BY WHICH I MYSELF HAVE BEEN LED AWAY, to believe in the possibility of instruction being so general as to destroy religious prejudices, which for a great number of unfortunate persons are a source of consolation.... The mass of the people, then, must be allowed its priests, its altars, and its public worship."

Blotted out for a moment, the old traditions had resumed their sway.

No example could better display the power of tradition on the mind of crowds. The most redoubtable idols do not dwell in temples, nor the most despotic tyrants in palaces; both the one and the other can be broken in an instant. But the invisible masters that reign in our innermost selves are safe from every effort at revolt, and only yield to the slow wearing away of centuries.

3. TIME

In social as in biological problems time is one of the most energetic factors. It is the sole real creator and the sole great destroyer. It is time that has made mountains with grains of sand and raised the obscure cell of geological eras to human dignity. The action of centuries is sufficient to transform any given phenomenon. It has been justly observed that an ant with enough time at its disposal could level Mount Blanc. A being possessed of the magical force of varying time at his will would have the power attributed by believers to God.

In this place, however, we have only to concern ourselves with the influence of time on the genesis of the opinions of crowds. Its action from this point of view is still immense. Dependent upon it are the great forces such as race, which cannot form themselves without it. It causes the birth, the growth, and the death of all beliefs. It is by the aid of time that they acquire their strength and also by its aid that they lose it.

It is time in particular that prepares the opinions and beliefs of crowds, or at least the soil on which they will germinate. This is why certain ideas are realisable at one epoch and not at another. It is time that accumulates that immense detritus of beliefs and thoughts on which the ideas of a given period spring up. They do not grow at hazard and by chance; the roots of each of them strike down into a long past. When they blossom it is time that has prepared their blooming; and to arrive at a notion of their genesis it is always back in the past that it is necessary to search. They are the daughters of the past and the mothers of the future, but throughout the slaves of time.

Time, in consequence, is our veritable master, and it suffices to leave it free to act to see all things transformed. At the present day we are very uneasy with regard to the threatening aspirations of the masses and the destructions and upheavals foreboded thereby. Time, without other aid, will see to the restoration of equilibrium. "No form of government," M. Lavisse very properly writes, "was founded in a day. Political and social organisations are works that demand centuries. The feudal system existed for centuries in a shapeless, chaotic state before it found its laws; absolute monarchy also existed for centuries before arriving at regular methods of government, and these periods of expectancy were extremely troubled."

4. POLITICAL AND SOCIAL INSTITUTIONS

The idea that institutions can remedy the defects of societies, that national progress is the consequence of the improvement of institutions and governments, and that social changes can be effected by decrees— this idea, I say, is still generally accepted. It was the starting-point of the French Revolution, and the social theories of the present day are based upon it.

The most continuous experience has been unsuccessful in shaking this grave delusion. Philosophers and historians have endeavoured in vain to prove its absurdity, but yet they have had no difficulty in demonstrating that institutions are the outcome of ideas, sentiments, and customs, and that ideas, sentiments, and customs are not to be recast by recasting legislative codes. A nation does not choose its institutions at will any more than it chooses the colour of its hair or its eyes. Institutions and governments are the product of the race. They are not the creators of an epoch, but are created by it. Peoples are not governed in accordance with their caprices of the moment, but as their character determines that they shall be governed. Centuries are required to form a political system and centuries needed to change it. Institutions have no intrinsic virtue: in themselves they are neither good nor bad. Those which are good at a given moment for a given people may be harmful in the extreme for another nation.

Moreover, it is in no way in the power of a people to really change its institutions. Undoubtedly, at the cost of violent revolutions, it can change their name, but in their essence they remain unmodified. The names are mere futile labels with which an historian who goes to the bottom of things need scarcely concern himself. It is in this way, for instance, that England, the most democratic country in the world, lives, nevertheless, under a monarchical regime, whereas the countries in which the most oppressive despotism is rampant are the Spanish-American Republics, in spite of their republican constitutions. The destinies of peoples are determined by their character and not by their government. I have endeavoured to establish this view in my previous volume by setting forth categorical examples.

"It should never be forgotten, even by the most ardent enemies of an aristocracy, that England is to-day the most democratic country of the universe, the country in which the rights of the individual are most respected, and in which the individual possesses the most liberty."

To lose time in the manufacture of cut-and-dried constitutions is, in consequence, a puerile task, the useless labour of an ignorant rhetorician. Necessity and time undertake the charge of elaborating constitutions when we are wise enough to allow these two factors to act. This is the plan the Anglo-Saxons have adopted, as their great historian, Macaulay, teaches us in a passage that the politicians of all Latin countries ought to learn by heart. After having shown all the good that can be accomplished by laws which appear from the point of view of pure reason a chaos of absurdities and contradictions, he compares the scores of constitutions that have been engulfed in the convulsions of the Latin peoples with that of England, and points out that the latter has only been very slowly changed part by part, under the influence of immediate necessities and never of speculative reasoning.

"To think nothing of symmetry and much of convenience; never to remove an anomaly merely because it is an anomaly; never to innovate except when some grievance is felt; never to innovate except so far as to get rid of the grievance; never to lay down any proposition of wider extent than the particular case for which it is necessary to provide; these are the rules which have, from the age of John to the age of Victoria, generally guided the deliberations of our two hundred and fifty Parliaments."

It would be necessary to take one by one the laws and institutions of each people to show to what extent they are the expression of the needs of each race and are incapable, for that reason, of being violently transformed. It is possible, for, instance, to indulge in philosophical dissertations on the advantages and disadvantages of centralisation; but when we see a people composed of very different races devote a thousand years of efforts to attaining to this centralisation; when we observe that a great revolution, having for object the destruction of all the institutions of the past, has been forced to respect this centralisation, and has even strengthened it; under these circumstances we should admit that it is the outcome of imperious needs, that it is a condition of the existence of the nation in question, and we should pity the poor mental range of politicians who talk of destroying it. Could they by chance succeed in this attempt, their success would at once be the signal for a frightful civil war, which, moreover, would immediately bring back a new system of centralisation much more oppressive than the old.

The conclusion to be drawn from what precedes is, that it is not in institutions that the means is to be sought of profoundly influencing the genius of the masses. When we see certain countries, such as the United States, reach a high degree of prosperity under democratic institutions, while others, such as the Spanish-American Republics, are found existing in a pitiable state of anarchy under absolutely similar institutions, we should admit that these institutions are as foreign to the greatness of the one as to the decadence of the others. Peoples are governed by their character, and all institutions which are not intimately modelled on that character merely represent a borrowed garment, a transitory disguise. No doubt sanguinary wars and violent revolutions have been undertaken, and will continue to be undertaken, to impose institutions to which is attributed, as to the relics of saints, the supernatural power of creating welfare. It may be said, then, in one sense, that institutions react on the mind of the crowd inasmuch as they engender such upheavals. But in reality it is not the institutions that react in this manner, since we know that, whether triumphant or vanquished, they possess in themselves no virtue. It is illusions and words that have influenced the mind of the crowd, and especially words— words which are as powerful as they are chimerical, and whose astonishing sway we shall shortly demonstrate.

5. INSTRUCTION AND EDUCATION

Foremost among the dominant ideas of the present epoch is to be found the notion that instruction is capable of considerably changing men, and has for its unfailing consequence to improve them and even to make them equal. By the mere fact of its being constantly repeated, this assertion has ended by becoming one of the most steadfast democratic dogmas. It would be as difficult now to attack it as it would have been formerly to have attacked the dogmas of the Church.

On this point, however, as on many others, democratic ideas are in profound disagreement with the results of psychology and experience. Many eminent philosophers, among them Herbert Spencer, have had no difficulty in showing that instruction neither renders a man more moral nor happier, that it changes neither his instincts nor his hereditary passions, and that at times—for this to happen it need only be badly directed—it is much more pernicious than useful. Statisticians have brought confirmation of these views by telling us that criminality increases with the generalisation of instruction, or at any rate of a certain kind of instruction, and that the worst enemies of society, the anarchists, are recruited among the prize-winners of schools; while in a recent work a distinguished magistrate, M. Adolphe Guillot, made the observation that at present 3,000 educated criminals are met with for every 1,000 illiterate delinquents, and that in fifty years the criminal percentage of the population has passed from 227 to 552 for every 100,000 inhabitants, an increase of 133 per cent. He has also noted in common with his colleagues that criminality is particularly on the increase among young persons, for whom, as is known, gratuitous and obligatory schooling has—in France—replaced apprenticeship.

It is not assuredly—and nobody has ever maintained this proposition— that well-directed instruction may not give very useful practical results, if not in the sense of raising the standard of morality, at least in that of developing professional capacity. Unfortunately the Latin peoples, especially in the last twenty-five years, have based their systems of instruction on very erroneous principles, and in spite of the observations of the most eminent minds, such as Breal, Fustel de Coulanges, Taine, and many others, they persist in their lamentable mistakes. I have myself shown, in a work published some time ago, that the French system of education transforms the majority of those who have undergone it into enemies of society, and recruits numerous disciples for the worst forms of socialism.

The primary danger of this system of education—very properly qualified as Latin—consists in the fact that it is based on the fundamental psychological error that the intelligence is developed by the learning by heart of text-books. Adopting this view, the endeavour has been made to enforce a knowledge of as many hand-books as possible. From the primary school till he leaves the university a young man does nothing but acquire books by heart without his judgment or personal initiative being ever called into play. Education consists for him in reciting by heart and obeying.

"Learning lessons, knowing by heart a grammar or a compendium, repeating well and imitating well—that," writes a former Minister of Public Instruction, M. Jules Simon, "is a ludicrous form of education whose every effort is an act of faith tacitly admitting the infallibility of the master, and whose only results are a belittling of ourselves and a rendering of us impotent."

Were this education merely useless, one might confine one's self to expressing compassion for the unhappy children who, instead of making needful studies at the primary school, are instructed in the genealogy of the sons of Clotaire, the conflicts between Neustria and Austrasia, or zoological classifications. But the system presents a far more serious danger. It gives those who have been submitted to it a violent dislike to the state of life in which they were born, and an intense desire to escape from it. The working man no longer wishes to remain a working man, or the peasant to continue a peasant, while the most humble members of the middle classes admit of no possible career for their sons except that of State-paid functionaries. Instead of preparing men for life French schools solely prepare them to occupy public functions, in which success can be attained without any necessity for self-direction or the exhibition of the least glimmer of personal initiative. At the bottom of the social ladder the system creates an army of proletarians discontented with their lot and always ready to revolt, while at the summit it brings into being a frivolous bourgeoisie, at once sceptical and credulous, having a superstitious confidence in the State, whom it regards as a sort of Providence, but without forgetting to display towards it a ceaseless hostility, always laying its own faults to the door of the Government, and incapable of the least enterprise without the intervention of the authorities.

The State, which manufactures by dint of textbooks all these persons possessing diplomas, can only utilise a small number of them, and is forced to leave the others without employment. It is obliged in consequence to resign itself to feeding the first mentioned and to having the others as its enemies. From the top to the bottom of the social pyramid, from the humblest clerk to the professor and the prefect, the immense mass of persons boasting diplomas besiege the professions. While a business man has the greatest difficulty in finding an agent to represent him in the colonies, thousands of candidates solicit the most modest official posts. There are 20,000 schoolmasters and mistresses without employment in the department of the Seine alone, all of them persons who, disdaining the fields or the workshops, look to the State for their livelihood. The number of the chosen being restricted, that of the discontented is perforce immense. The latter are ready for any revolution, whoever be its chiefs and whatever the goal they aim at. The acquisition of knowledge for which no use can be found is a sure method of driving a man to revolt.

It is evidently too late to retrace our steps. Experience alone, that supreme educator of peoples, will be at pains to show us our mistake. It alone will be powerful enough to prove the necessity of replacing our odious text-books and our pitiable examinations by industrial instruction capable of inducing our young men to return to the fields, to the workshop, and to the colonial enterprise which they avoid to-day at all costs.

The professional instruction which all enlightened minds are now demanding was the instruction received in the past by our forefathers. It is still in vigour at the present day among the nations who rule the world by their force of will, their initiative, and their spirit of enterprise. In a series of remarkable pages, whose principal passages I reproduce further on, a great thinker, M. Taine, has clearly shown that our former system of education was approximately that in vogue to-day in England and America, and in a remarkable parallel between the Latin and Anglo-Saxon systems he has plainly pointed out the consequences of the two methods.

One might consent, perhaps, at a pinch, to continue to accept all the disadvantages of our classical education, although it produced nothing but discontented men, and men unfitted for their station in life, did the superficial acquisition of so much knowledge, the faultless repeating by heart of so many text-books, raise the level of intelligence. But does it really raise this level? Alas, no! The conditions of success in life are the possession of judgment, experience, initiative, and character—qualities which are not bestowed by books. Books are dictionaries, which it is useful to consult, but of which it is perfectly useless to have lengthy portions in one's head.

How is it possible for professional instruction to develop the intelligence in a measure quite beyond the reach of classical instruction? This has been well shown by M. Taine.

"Ideas, he says, are only formed in their natural and normal surroundings; the promotion of the growth is effected by the innumerable impressions appealing to the senses which a young man receives daily in the workshop, the mine, the law court, the study, the builder's yard, the hospital; at the sight of tools, materials, and operations; in the presence of customers, workers, and labour, of work well or ill done, costly or lucrative. In such a way are obtained those trifling perceptions of detail of the eyes, the ear, the hands, and even the sense of smell, which, picked up involuntarily, and silently elaborated, take shape within the learner, and suggest to him sooner or, later this or that new combination, simplification, economy, improvement, or invention. The young Frenchman is deprived, and precisely at the age when they are most fruitful, of all these precious contacts, of all these indispensable elements of assimilation. For seven or eight years on end he is shut up in a school, and is cut off from that direct personal experience which would give him a keen and exact notion of men and things and of the various ways of handling them."

"... At least nine out of ten have wasted their time and pains during several years of their life—telling, important, even decisive years. Among such are to be counted, first of all, the half or two-thirds of those who present themselves for examination—I refer to those who are rejected; and then among those who are successful, who obtain a degree, a certificate, a diploma, there is still a half or two-thirds—I refer to the overworked. Too much has been demanded of them by exacting that on a given day, on a chair or before a board, they should, for two hours in succession, and with respect to a group of sciences, be living repertories of all human knowledge. In point of fact they were that, or nearly so, for two hours on that particular day, but a month later they are so no longer. They could not go through the examination again. Their too numerous and too burdensome acquisitions slip incessantly from their mind, and are not replaced. Their mental vigour has declined, their fertile capacity for growth has dried up, the fully-developed man appears, and he is often a used-up man. Settled down, married, resigned to turning in a circle, and indefinitely in the same circle, he shuts himself up in his confined function, which he fulfils adequately, but nothing more. Such is the average yield: assuredly the receipts do not balance the expenditure. In England or America, where, as in France previous to 1789, the contrary proceeding is adopted, the outcome obtained is equal or superior."

The illustrious psychologist subsequently shows us the difference between our system and that of the Anglo-Saxons. The latter do not possess our innumerable special schools. With them instruction is not based on book-learning, but on object lessons. The engineer, for example, is trained in a workshop, and never at a school; a method which allows of each individual reaching the level his intelligence permits of. He becomes a workman or a foreman if he can get no further, an engineer if his aptitudes take him as far. This manner of proceeding is much more democratic and of much greater benefit to society than that of making the whole career of an individual depend on an examination, lasting a few hours, and undergone at the age of nineteen or twenty.

"In the hospital, the mine, the factory, in the architect's or the lawyer's office, the student, who makes a start while very young, goes through his apprenticeship, stage by stage, much as does with us a law clerk in his office, or an artist in his studio. Previously, and before making a practical beginning, he has had an opportunity of following some general and summary course of instruction, so as to have a framework ready prepared in which to store the observations he is shortly to make. Furthermore he is able, as a rule, to avail himself of sundry technical courses which he can follow in his leisure hours, so as to co-ordinate step by step the daily experience he is gathering. Under such a system the practical capabilities increase and develop of themselves in exact proportion to the faculties of the student, and in the direction requisite for his future task and the special work for which from now onwards he desires to fit himself. By this means in England or the United States a young man is quickly in a position to develop his capacity to the utmost. At twenty-five years of age, and much sooner if the material and the parts are there, he is not merely a useful performer, he is capable also of spontaneous enterprise; he is not only a part of a machine, but also a motor. In France, where the contrary system prevails—in France, which with each succeeding generation is falling more and more into line with China—the sum total of the wasted forces is enormous."

The great philosopher arrives at the following conclusion with respect to the growing incongruity between our Latin system of education and the requirements of practical life:—

"In the three stages of instruction, those of childhood, adolescence and youth, the theoretical and pedagogic preparation by books on the school benches has lengthened out and become overcharged in view of the examination, the degree, the diploma, and the certificate, and solely in this view, and by the worst methods, by the application of an unnatural and anti-social regime, by the excessive postponement of the practical apprenticeship, by our boarding-school system, by artificial training and mechanical cramming, by overwork, without thought for the time that is to follow, for the adult age and the functions of the man, without regard for the real world on which the young man will shortly be thrown, for the society in which we move and to which he must be adapted or be taught to resign himself in advance, for the struggle in which humanity is engaged, and in which to defend himself and to keep his footing he ought previously to have been equipped, armed, trained, and hardened. This indispensable equipment, this acquisition of more importance than any other, this sturdy common sense and nerve and will-power our schools do not procure the young Frenchman; on the contrary, far from qualifying him for his approaching and definite state, they disqualify him. In consequence, his entry into the world and his first steps in the field of action are most often merely a succession of painful falls, whose effect is that he long remains wounded and bruised, and sometimes disabled for life. The test is severe and dangerous. In the course of it the mental and moral equilibrium is affected, and runs the risk of not being re-established. Too sudden and complete disillusion has supervened. The deceptions have been too great, the disappointments too keen."

A useful comparison may be made between Taine's pages and the observations on American education recently made by M. Paul Bourget in his excellent book, "Outre-Mer." He, too, after having noted that our education merely produces narrow-minded bourgeois, lacking in initiative and will-power, or anarchists—"those two equally harmful types of the civilised man, who degenerates into impotent platitude or insane destructiveness"—he too, I say, draws a comparison that cannot be the object of too much reflection between our French lycees (public schools), those factories of degeneration, and the American schools, which prepare a man admirably for life. The gulf existing between truly democratic nations and those who have democracy in their speeches, but in no wise in their thoughts, is clearly brought out in this comparison.

Have we digressed in what precedes from the psychology of crowds? Assuredly not. If we desire to understand the ideas and beliefs that are germinating to-day in the masses, and will spring up to-morrow, it is necessary to know how the ground has been prepared. The instruction given the youth of a country allows of a knowledge of what that country will one day be. The education accorded the present generation justifies the most gloomy previsions. It is in part by instruction and education that the mind of the masses is improved or deteriorated. It was necessary in consequence to show how this mind has been fashioned by the system in vogue, and how the mass of the indifferent and the neutral has become progressively an army of the discontented ready to obey all the suggestions of utopians and rhetoricians. It is in the schoolroom that socialists and anarchists are found nowadays, and that the way is being paved for the approaching period of decadence for the Latin peoples.

CHAPTER II: THE IMMEDIATE FACTORS OF THE OPINIONS OF CROWDS

1. IMAGES, WORDS AND FORMULAE. The magical power of words and formulae—The power of words bound up with the images they evoke, and independent of their real sense—These images vary from age to age, and from race to race—The wear and tear of words—Examples of the considerable variations of sense of much-used words—The political utility of baptizing old things with new names when the words by which they were designated produced an unfavourable impression on the masses— variations of the sense of words in consequence of race differences—The different meanings of the word "democracy" in Europe and America. 2. ILLUSIONS. Their importance—They are to be found at the root of all civilisations—The social necessity of illusions—Crowds always prefer them to truths. 3. EXPERIENCE. Experience alone can fix in the mind of crowds truths become necessary and destroy illusions grown dangerous—Experience is only effective on the condition that it be frequently repeated—The cost of the experiences requisite to persuade crowds. 4. REASON. The nullity of its influence on crowds—Crowds only to be influenced by their unconscious sentiments— The role of logic in history—The secret causes of improbable events.

We have just investigated the remote and preparatory factors which give the mind of crowds a special receptivity, and make possible therein the growth of certain sentiments and certain ideas. It now remains for us to study the factors capable of acting in a direct manner. We shall see in a forthcoming chapter how these factors should be put in force in order that they may produce their full effect.

In the first part of this work we studied the sentiments, ideas, and methods of reasoning of collective bodies, and from the knowledge thus acquired it would evidently be possible to deduce in a general way the means of making an impression on their mind. We already know what strikes the imagination of crowds, and are acquainted with the power and contagiousness of suggestions, of those especially that are presented under the form of images. However, as suggestions may proceed from very different sources, the factors capable of acting on the minds of crowds may differ considerably. It is necessary, then, to study them separately. This is not a useless study. Crowds are somewhat like the sphinx of ancient fable: it is necessary to arrive at a solution of the problems offered by their psychology or to resign ourselves to being devoured by them.

1. IMAGES, WORDS, AND FORMULAS

When studying the imagination of crowds we saw that it is particularly open to the impressions produced by images. These images do not always lie ready to hand, but it is possible to evoke them by the judicious employment of words and formulas. Handled with art, they possess in sober truth the mysterious power formerly attributed to them by the adepts of magic. They cause the birth in the minds of crowds of the most formidable tempests, which in turn they are capable of stilling. A pyramid far loftier than that of old Cheops could be raised merely with the bones of men who have been victims of the power of words and formulas.

The power of words is bound up with the images they evoke, and is quite independent of their real significance. Words whose sense is the most ill-defined are sometimes those that possess the most influence. Such, for example, are the terms democracy, socialism, equality, liberty, &c., whose meaning is so vague that bulky volumes do not suffice to precisely fix it. Yet it is certain that a truly magical power is attached to those short syllables, as if they contained the solution of all problems. They synthesise the most diverse unconscious aspirations and the hope of their realisation.

Reason and arguments are incapable of combatting certain words and formulas. They are uttered with solemnity in the presence of crowds, and as soon as they have been pronounced an expression of respect is visible on every countenance, and all heads are bowed. By many they are considered as natural forces, as supernatural powers. They evoke grandiose and vague images in men's minds, but this very vagueness that wraps them in obscurity augments their mysterious power. They are the mysterious divinities hidden behind the tabernacle, which the devout only approach in fear and trembling.

The images evoked by words being independent of their sense, they vary from age to age and from people to people, the formulas remaining identical. Certain transitory images are attached to certain words: the word is merely as it were the button of an electric bell that calls them up.

All words and all formulas do not possess the power of evoking images, while there are some which have once had this power, but lose it in the course of use, and cease to waken any response in the mind. They then become vain sounds, whose principal utility is to relieve the person who employs them of the obligation of thinking. Armed with a small stock of formulas and commonplaces learnt while we are young, we possess all that is needed to traverse life without the tiring necessity of having to reflect on anything whatever.

If any particular language be studied, it is seen that the words of which it is composed change rather slowly in the course of ages, while the images these words evoke or the meaning attached to them changes ceaselessly. This is the reason why, in another work, I have arrived at the conclusion that the absolute translation of a language, especially of a dead language, is totally impossible. What do we do in reality when we substitute a French for a Latin, Greek, or Sanscrit expression, or even when we endeavour to understand a book written in our own tongue two or three centuries back? We merely put the images and ideas with which modern life has endowed our intelligence in the place of absolutely distinct notions and images which ancient life had brought into being in the mind of races submitted to conditions of existence having no analogy with our own. When the men of the Revolution imagined they were copying the Greeks and Romans, what were they doing except giving to ancient words a sense the latter had never had? What resemblance can possibly exist between the institutions of the Greeks and those designated to-day by corresponding words? A republic at that epoch was an essentially aristocratic institution, formed of a reunion of petty despots ruling over a crowd of slaves kept in the most absolute subjection. These communal aristocracies, based on slavery, could not have existed for a moment without it.

The word "liberty," again, what signification could it have in any way resembling that we attribute to it to-day at a period when the possibility of the liberty of thought was not even suspected, and when there was no greater and more exceptional crime than that of discussing the gods, the laws and the customs of the city? What did such a word as "fatherland" signify to an Athenian or Spartan unless it were the cult of Athens or Sparta, and in no wise that of Greece, composed of rival cities always at war with each other? What meaning had the same word "fatherland" among the ancient Gauls, divided into rival tribes and races, and possessing different languages and religions, and who were easily vanquished by Caesar because he always found allies among them? It was Rome that made a country of Gaul by endowing it with political and religious unity. Without going back so far, scarcely two centuries ago, is it to be believed that this same notion of a fatherland was conceived to have the same meaning as at present by French princes like the great Conde, who allied themselves with the foreigner against their sovereign? And yet again, the same word had it not a sense very different from the modern for the French royalist emigrants, who thought they obeyed the laws of honour in fighting against France, and who from their point of view did indeed obey them, since the feudal law bound the vassal to the lord and not to the soil, so that where the sovereign was there was the true fatherland?

Numerous are the words whose meaning has thus profoundly changed from age to age—words which we can only arrive at understanding in the sense in which they were formerly understood after a long effort. It has been said with truth that much study is necessary merely to arrive at conceiving what was signified to our great grandfathers by such words as the "king" and the "royal family." What, then, is likely to be the case with terms still more complex?

Words, then, have only mobile and transitory significations which change from age to age and people to people; and when we desire to exert an influence by their means on the crowd what it is requisite to know is the meaning given them by the crowd at a given moment, and not the meaning which they formerly had or may yet have for individuals of a different mental constitution.

Thus, when crowds have come, as the result of political upheavals or changes of belief, to acquire a profound antipathy for the images evoked by certain words, the first duty of the true statesman is to change the words without, of course, laying hands on the things themselves, the latter being too intimately bound up with the inherited constitution to be transformed. The judicious Tocqueville long ago made the remark that the work of the consulate and the empire consisted more particularly in the clothing with new words of the greater part of the institutions of the past—that is to say, in replacing words evoking disagreeable images in the imagination of the crowd by other words of which the novelty prevented such evocations. The "taille" or tallage has become the land tax; the "gabelle," the tax on salt; the "aids," the indirect contributions and the consolidated duties; the tax on trade companies and guilds, the license, &c.

One of the most essential functions of statesmen consists, then, in baptizing with popular or, at any rate, indifferent words things the crowd cannot endure under their old names. The power of words is so great that it suffices to designate in well-chosen terms the most odious things to make them acceptable to crowds. Taine justly observes that it was by invoking liberty and fraternity—words very popular at the time— that the Jacobins were able "to install a despotism worthy of Dahomey, a tribunal similar to that of the Inquisition, and to accomplish human hecatombs akin to those of ancient Mexico." The art of those who govern, as is the case with the art of advocates, consists above all in the science of employing words. One of the greatest difficulties of this art is, that in one and the same society the same words most often have very different meanings for the different social classes, who employ in appearance the same words, but never speak the same language.

In the preceding examples it is especially time that has been made to intervene as the principal factor in the changing of the meaning of words. If, however, we also make race intervene, we shall then see that, at the same period, among peoples equally civilised but of different race, the same words very often correspond to extremely dissimilar ideas. It is impossible to understand these differences without having travelled much, and for this reason I shall not insist upon them. I shall confine myself to observing that it is precisely the words most often employed by the masses which among different peoples possess the most different meanings. Such is the case, for instance, with the words "democracy" and "socialism" in such frequent use nowadays.

In reality they correspond to quite contrary ideas and images in the Latin and Anglo-Saxon mind. For the Latin peoples the word "democracy" signifies more especially the subordination of the will and the initiative of the individual to the will and the initiative of the community represented by the State. It is the State that is charged, to a greater and greater degree, with the direction of everything, the centralisation, the monopolisation, and the manufacture of everything. To the State it is that all parties without exception, radicals, socialists, or monarchists, constantly appeal. Among the Anglo-Saxons and notably in America this same word "democracy" signifies, on the contrary, the intense development of the will of the individual, and as complete a subordination as possible of the State, which, with the exception of the police, the army, and diplomatic relations, is not allowed the direction of anything, not even of public instruction. It is seen, then, that the same word which signifies for one people the subordination of the will and the initiative of the individual and the preponderance of the State, signifies for another the excessive development of the will and the initiative of the individual and the complete subordination of the State.

2. ILLUSIONS

From the dawn of civilisation onwards crowds have always undergone the influence of illusions. It is to the creators of illusions that they have raised more temples, statues, and altars than to any other class of men. Whether it be the religious illusions of the past or the philosophic and social illusions of the present, these formidable sovereign powers are always found at the head of all the civilisations that have successively flourished on our planet. It is in their name that were built the temples of Chaldea and Egypt and the religious edifices of the Middle Ages, and that a vast upheaval shook the whole of Europe a century ago, and there is not one of our political, artistic, or social conceptions that is free from their powerful impress. Occasionally, at the cost of terrible disturbances, man overthrows them, but he seems condemned to always set them up again. Without them he would never have emerged from his primitive barbarian state, and without them again he would soon return to it. Doubtless they are futile shadows; but these children of our dreams have forced the nations to create whatever the arts may boast of splendour or civilisation of greatness.

"If one destroyed in museums and libraries, if one hurled down on the flagstones before the churches all the works and all the monuments of art that religions have inspired, what would remain of the great dreams of humanity? To give to men that portion of hope and illusion without which they cannot live, such is the reason for the existence of gods, heroes, and poets. During fifty years science appeared to undertake this task. But science has been compromised in hearts hungering after the ideal, because it does not dare to be lavish enough of promises, because it cannot lie."

The philosophers of the last century devoted themselves with fervour to the destruction of the religious, political, and social illusions on which our forefathers had lived for a long tale of centuries. By destroying them they have dried up the springs of hope and resignation. Behind the immolated chimeras they came face to face with the blind and silent forces of nature, which are inexorable to weakness and ignore pity.

Notwithstanding all its progress, philosophy has been unable as yet to offer the masses any ideal that can charm them; but, as they must have their illusions at all cost, they turn instinctively, as the insect seeks the light, to the rhetoricians who accord them what they want. Not truth, but error has always been the chief factor in the evolution of nations, and the reason why socialism is so powerful to-day is that it constitutes the last illusion that is still vital. In spite of all scientific demonstrations it continues on the increase. Its principal strength lies in the fact that it is championed by minds sufficiently ignorant of things as they are in reality to venture boldly to promise mankind happiness. The social illusion reigns to-day upon all the heaped-up ruins of the past, and to it belongs the future. The masses have never thirsted after truth. They turn aside from evidence that is not to their taste, preferring to deify error, if error seduce them. Whoever can supply them with illusions is easily their master; whoever attempts to destroy their illusions is always their victim.

3. EXPERIENCE

Experience constitutes almost the only effective process by which a truth may be solidly established in the mind of the masses, and illusions grown too dangerous be destroyed. To this end, however, it is necessary that the experience should take place on a very large scale, and be very frequently repeated. The experiences undergone by one generation are useless, as a rule, for the generation that follows, which is the reason why historical facts, cited with a view to demonstration, serve no purpose. Their only utility is to prove to what an extent experiences need to be repeated from age to age to exert any influence, or to be successful in merely shaking an erroneous opinion when it is solidly implanted in the mind of the masses.

Our century and that which preceded it will doubtless be alluded to by historians as an era of curious experiments, which in no other age have been tried in such number.

The most gigantic of these experiments was the French Revolution. To find out that a society is not to be refashioned from top to bottom in accordance with the dictates of pure reason, it was necessary that several millions of men should be massacred and that Europe should be profoundly disturbed for a period of twenty years. To prove to us experimentally that dictators cost the nations who acclaim them dear, two ruinous experiences have been required in fifty years, and in spite of their clearness they do not seem to have been sufficiently convincing. The first, nevertheless, cost three millions of men and an invasion, the second involved a loss of territory, and carried in its wake the necessity for permanent armies. A third was almost attempted not long since, and will assuredly be attempted one day. To bring an entire nation to admit that the huge German army was not, as was currently alleged thirty years ago, a sort of harmless national guard, the terrible war which cost us so dear had to take place. To bring about the recognition that Protection ruins the nations who adopt it, at least twenty years of disastrous experience will be needful. These examples might be indefinitely multiplied.

4. REASON

In enumerating the factors capable of making an impression on the minds of crowds all mention of reason might be dispensed with, were it not necessary to point out the negative value of its influence.

We have already shown that crowds are not to be influenced by reasoning, and can only comprehend rough-and-ready associations of ideas. The orators who know how to make an impression upon them always appeal in consequence to their sentiments and never to their reason. The laws of logic have no action on crowds. To bring home conviction to crowds it is necessary first of all to thoroughly comprehend the sentiments by which they are animated, to pretend to share these sentiments, then to endeavour to modify them by calling up, by means of rudimentary associations, certain eminently suggestive notions, to be capable, if need be, of going back to the point of view from which a start was made, and, above all, to divine from instant to instant the sentiments to which one's discourse is giving birth. This necessity of ceaselessly varying one's language in accordance with the effect produced at the moment of speaking deprives from the outset a prepared and studied harangue of all efficaciousness. In such a speech the orator follows his own line of thought, not that of his hearers, and from this fact alone his influence is annihilated.

Logical minds, accustomed to be convinced by a chain of somewhat close reasoning, cannot avoid having recourse to this mode of persuasion when addressing crowds, and the inability of their arguments always surprises them. "The usual mathematical consequences based on the syllogism—that is, on associations of identities—are imperative..." writes a logician. "This imperativeness would enforce the assent even of an inorganic mass were it capable of following associations of identities." This is doubtless true, but a crowd is no more capable than an inorganic mass of following such associations, nor even of understanding them. If the attempt be made to convince by reasoning primitive minds—savages or children, for instance—the slight value possessed by this method of arguing will be understood.

It is not even necessary to descend so low as primitive beings to obtain an insight into the utter powerlessness of reasoning when it has to fight against sentiment. Let us merely call to mind how tenacious, for centuries long, have been religious superstitions in contradiction with the simplest logic. For nearly two thousand years the most luminous geniuses have bowed before their laws, and modern times have to be reached for their veracity to be merely contested. The Middle Ages and the Renaissance possessed many enlightened men, but not a single man who attained by reasoning to an appreciation of the childish side of his superstitions, or who promulgated even a slight doubt as to the misdeeds of the devil or the necessity of burning sorcerers.

Should it be regretted that crowds are never guided by reason? We would not venture to affirm it. Without a doubt human reason would not have availed to spur humanity along the path of civilisation with the ardour and hardihood its illusions have done. These illusions, the offspring of those unconscious forces by which we are led, were doubtless necessary. Every race carries in its mental constitution the laws of its destiny, and it is, perhaps, these laws that it obeys with a resistless impulse, even in the case of those of its impulses which apparently are the most unreasoned. It seems at times as if nations were submitted to secret forces analogous to those which compel the acorn to transform itself into an oak or a comet to follow its orbit.

What little insight we can get into these forces must be sought for in the general course of the evolution of a people, and not in the isolated facts from which this evolution appears at times to proceed. Were these facts alone to be taken into consideration, history would seem to be the result of a series of improbable chances. It was improbable that a Galilean carpenter should become for two thousand years an all-powerful God in whose name the most important civilisations were founded; improbable, too, that a few bands of Arabs, emerging from their deserts, should conquer the greater part of the old Graco-Roman world, and establish an empire greater than that of Alexander; improbable, again, that in Europe, at an advanced period of its development, and when authority throughout it had been systematically hierarchised, an obscure lieutenant of artillery should have succeeded in reigning over a multitude of peoples and kings.

Let us leave reason, then, to philosophers, and not insist too strongly on its intervention in the governing of men. It is not by reason, but most often in spite of it, that are created those sentiments that are the mainsprings of all civilisation—sentiments such as honour, self- sacrifice, religious faith, patriotism, and the love of glory.

CHAPTER III: THE LEADERS OF CROWDS AND THEIR MEANS OF PERSUASION

1. THE LEADERS OF CROWDS. The instinctive need of all beings forming a crowd to obey a leader—The psychology of the leaders of crowds—They alone can endow crowds with faith and organise them—The leaders forcibly despotic—Classification of the leaders—The part played by the will. 2. THE MEANS OF ACTION OF THE LEADERS. Affirmation, repetition, contagion—The respective part of these different factors—The way in which contagion may spread from the lower to the upper classes in a society—A popular opinion soon becomes a general opinion. 3. PRESTIGE. Definition of prestige and classification of its different kinds—Acquired prestige and personal prestige—Various examples—The way in which prestige is destroyed.

We are now acquainted with the mental constitution of crowds, and we also know what are the motives capable of making an impression on their mind. It remains to investigate how these motives may be set in action, and by whom they may usefully be turned to practical account.

1. THE LEADERS OF CROWDS

As soon as a certain number of living beings are gathered together, whether they be animals or men, they place themselves instinctively under the authority of a chief.

In the case of human crowds the chief is often nothing more than a ringleader or agitator, but as such he plays a considerable part. His will is the nucleus around which the opinions of the crowd are grouped and attain to identity. He constitutes the first element towards the organisation of heterogeneous crowds, and paves the way for their organisation in sects; in the meantime he directs them. A crowd is a servile flock that is incapable of ever doing without a master.

The leader has most often started as one of the led. He has himself been hypnotised by the idea, whose apostle he has since become. It has taken possession of him to such a degree that everything outside it vanishes, and that every contrary opinion appears to him an error or a superstition. An example in point is Robespierre, hypnotised by the philosophical ideas of Rousseau, and employing the methods of the Inquisition to propagate them.

The leaders we speak of are more frequently men of action than thinkers. They are not gifted with keen foresight, nor could they be, as this quality generally conduces to doubt and inactivity. They are especially recruited from the ranks of those morbidly nervous, excitable, half-deranged persons who are bordering on madness. However absurd may be the idea they uphold or the goal they pursue, their convictions are so strong that all reasoning is lost upon them. Contempt and persecution do not affect them, or only serve to excite them the more. They sacrifice their personal interest, their family—everything. The very instinct of self-preservation is entirely obliterated in them, and so much so that often the only recompense they solicit is that of martyrdom. The intensity of their faith gives great power of suggestion to their words. The multitude is always ready to listen to the strong-willed man, who knows how to impose himself upon it. Men gathered in a crowd lose all force of will, and turn instinctively to the person who possesses the quality they lack.

Nations have never lacked leaders, but all of the latter have by no means been animated by those strong convictions proper to apostles. These leaders are often subtle rhetoricians, seeking only their own personal interest, and endeavouring to persuade by flattering base instincts. The influence they can assert in this manner may be very great, but it is always ephemeral. The men of ardent convictions who have stirred the soul of crowds, the Peter the Hermits, the Luthers, the Savonarolas, the men of the French Revolution, have only exercised their fascination after having been themselves fascinated first of all by a creed. They are then able to call up in the souls of their fellows that formidable force known as faith, which renders a man the absolute slave of his dream.

The arousing of faith—whether religious, political, or social, whether faith in a work, in a person, or an idea—has always been the function of the great leaders of crowds, and it is on this account that their influence is always very great. Of all the forces at the disposal of humanity, faith has always been one of the most tremendous, and the gospel rightly attributes to it the power of moving mountains. To endow a man with faith is to multiply his strength tenfold. The great events of history have been brought about by obscure believers, who have had little beyond their faith in their favour. It is not by the aid of the learned or of philosophers, and still less of sceptics, that have been built up the great religions which have swayed the world, or the vast empires which have spread from one hemisphere to the other.

In the cases just cited, however, we are dealing with great leaders, and they are so few in number that history can easily reckon them up. They form the summit of a continuous series, which extends from these powerful masters of men down to the workman who, in the smoky atmosphere of an inn, slowly fascinates his comrades by ceaselessly drumming into their ears a few set phrases, whose purport he scarcely comprehends, but the application of which, according to him, must surely bring about the realisation of all dreams and of every hope.

In every social sphere, from the highest to the lowest, as soon as a man ceases to be isolated he speedily falls under the influence of a leader. The majority of men, especially among the masses, do not possess clear and reasoned ideas on any subject whatever outside their own speciality. The leader serves them as guide. It is just possible that he may be replaced, though very inefficiently, by the periodical publications which manufacture opinions for their readers and supply them with ready- made phrases which dispense them of the trouble of reasoning.

The leaders of crowds wield a very despotic authority, and this despotism indeed is a condition of their obtaining a following. It has often been remarked how easily they extort obedience, although without any means of backing up their authority, from the most turbulent section of the working classes. They fix the hours of labour and the rate of wages, and they decree strikes, which are begun and ended at the hour they ordain.

At the present day these leaders and agitators tend more and more to usurp the place of the public authorities in proportion as the latter allow themselves to be called in question and shorn of their strength. The tyranny of these new masters has for result that the crowds obey them much more docilely than they have obeyed any government. If in consequence of some accident or other the leaders should be removed from the scene the crowd returns to its original state of a collectivity without cohesion or force of resistance. During the last strike of the Parisian omnibus employes the arrest of the two leaders who were directing it was at once sufficient to bring it to an end. It is the need not of liberty but of servitude that is always predominant in the soul of crowds. They are so bent on obedience that they instinctively submit to whoever declares himself their master.

These ringleaders and agitators may be divided into two clearly defined classes. The one includes the men who are energetic and possess, but only intermittently, much strength of will, the other the men, far rarer than the preceding, whose strength of will is enduring. The first mentioned are violent, brave, and audacious. They are more especially useful to direct a violent enterprise suddenly decided on, to carry the masses with them in spite of danger, and to transform into heroes the men who but yesterday were recruits. Men of this kind were Ney and Murat under the First Empire, and such a man in our own time was Garibaldi, a talentless but energetic adventurer who succeeded with a handful of men in laying hands on the ancient kingdom of Naples, defended though it was by a disciplined army.

Still, though the energy of leaders of this class is a force to be reckoned with, it is transitory, and scarcely outlasts the exciting cause that has brought it into play. When they have returned to their ordinary course of life the heroes animated by energy of this description often evince, as was the case with those I have just cited, the most astonishing weakness of character. They seem incapable of reflection and of conducting themselves under the simplest circumstances, although they had been able to lead others. These men are leaders who cannot exercise their function except on the condition that they be led themselves and continually stimulated, that they have always as their beacon a man or an idea, that they follow a line of conduct clearly traced. The second category of leaders, that of men of enduring strength of will, have, in spite of a less brilliant aspect, a much more considerable influence. In this category are to be found the true founders of religions and great undertakings: St. Paul, Mahomet, Christopher Columbus, and de Lesseps, for example. Whether they be intelligent or narrow-minded is of no importance: the world belongs to them. The persistent will-force they possess is an immensely rare and immensely powerful faculty to which everything yields. What a strong and continuous will is capable of is not always properly appreciated. Nothing resists it; neither nature, gods, nor man.

The most recent example of what can be effected by a strong and continuous will is afforded us by the illustrious man who separated the Eastern and Western worlds, and accomplished a task that during three thousand years had been attempted in vain by the greatest sovereigns. He failed later in an identical enterprise, but then had intervened old age, to which everything, even the will, succumbs.

When it is desired to show what may be done by mere strength of will, all that is necessary is to relate in detail the history of the difficulties that had to be surmounted in connection with the cutting of the Suez Canal. An ocular witness, Dr. Cazalis, has summed up in a few striking lines the entire story of this great work, recounted by its immortal author.

"From day to day, episode by episode, he told the stupendous story of the canal. He told of all he had had to vanquish, of the impossible he had made possible, of all the opposition he encountered, of the coalition against him, and the disappointments, the reverses, the defeats which had been unavailing to discourage or depress him. He recalled how England had combatted him, attacking him without cessation, how Egypt and France had hesitated, how the French Consul had been foremost in his opposition to the early stages of the work, and the nature of the opposition he had met with, the attempt to force his workmen to desert from thirst by refusing them fresh water; how the Minister of Marine and the engineers, all responsible men of experienced and scientific training, had naturally all been hostile, were all certain on scientific grounds that disaster was at hand, had calculated its coming, foretelling it for such a day and hour as an eclipse is foretold."

The book which relates the lives of all these great leaders would not contain many names, but these names have been bound up with the most important events in the history of civilisation.

2. THE MEANS OF ACTION OF THE LEADERS: AFFIRMATION, REPETITION, CONTAGION

When it is wanted to stir up a crowd for a short space of time, to induce it to commit an act of any nature—to pillage a palace, or to die in defence of a stronghold or a barricade, for instance—the crowd must be acted upon by rapid suggestion, among which example is the most powerful in its effect. To attain this end, however, it is necessary that the crowd should have been previously prepared by certain circumstances, and, above all, that he who wishes to work upon it should possess the quality to be studied farther on, to which I give the name of prestige.

When, however, it is proposed to imbue the mind of a crowd with ideas and beliefs—with modern social theories, for instance—the leaders have recourse to different expedients. The principal of them are three in number and clearly defined—affirmation, repetition, and contagion. Their action is somewhat slow, but its effects, once produced, are very lasting.

Affirmation pure and simple, kept free of all reasoning and all proof, is one of the surest means of making an idea enter the mind of crowds. The conciser an affirmation is, the more destitute of every appearance of proof and demonstration, the more weight it carries. The religious books and the legal codes of all ages have always resorted to simple affirmation. Statesmen called upon to defend a political cause, and commercial men pushing the sale of their products by means of advertising are acquainted with the value of affirmation.

Affirmation, however, has no real influence unless it be constantly repeated, and so far as possible in the same terms. It was Napoleon, I believe, who said that there is only one figure in rhetoric of serious importance, namely, repetition. The thing affirmed comes by repetition to fix itself in the mind in such a way that it is accepted in the end as a demonstrated truth.

The influence of repetition on crowds is comprehensible when the power is seen which it exercises on the most enlightened minds. This power is due to the fact that the repeated statement is embedded in the long run in those profound regions of our unconscious selves in which the motives of our actions are forged. At the end of a certain time we have forgotten who is the author of the repeated assertion, and we finish by believing it. To this circumstance is due the astonishing power of advertisements. When we have read a hundred, a thousand, times that X's chocolate is the best, we imagine we have heard it said in many quarters, and we end by acquiring the certitude that such is the fact. When we have read a thousand times that Y's flour has cured the most illustrious persons of the most obstinate maladies, we are tempted at last to try it when suffering from an illness of a similar kind. If we always read in the same papers that A is an arrant scamp and B a most honest man we finish by being convinced that this is the truth, unless, indeed, we are given to reading another paper of the contrary opinion, in which the two qualifications are reversed. Affirmation and repetition are alone powerful enough to combat each other.

When an affirmation has been sufficiently repeated and there is unanimity in this repetition—as has occurred in the case of certain famous financial undertakings rich enough to purchase every assistance— what is called a current of opinion is formed and the powerful mechanism of contagion intervenes. Ideas, sentiments, emotions, and beliefs possess in crowds a contagious power as intense as that of microbes. This phenomenon is very natural, since it is observed even in animals when they are together in number. Should a horse in a stable take to biting his manger the other horses in the stable will imitate him. A panic that has seized on a few sheep will soon extend to the whole flock. In the case of men collected in a crowd all emotions are very rapidly contagious, which explains the suddenness of panics. Brain disorders, like madness, are themselves contagious. The frequency of madness among doctors who are specialists for the mad is notorious. Indeed, forms of madness have recently been cited—agoraphobia, for instance—which are communicable from men to animals.

For individuals to succumb to contagion their simultaneous presence on the same spot is not indispensable. The action of contagion may be felt from a distance under the influence of events which give all minds an individual trend and the characteristics peculiar to crowds. This is especially the case when men's minds have been prepared to undergo the influence in question by those remote factors of which I have made a study above. An example in point is the revolutionary movement of 1848, which, after breaking out in Paris, spread rapidly over a great part of Europe and shook a number of thrones.

Imitation, to which so much influence is attributed in social phenomena, is in reality a mere effect of contagion. Having shown its influence elsewhere, I shall confine myself to reproducing what I said on the subject fifteen years ago. My remarks have since been developed by other writers in recent publications.

"Man, like animals, has a natural tendency to imitation. Imitation is a necessity for him, provided always that the imitation is quite easy. It is this necessity that makes the influence of what is called fashion so powerful. Whether in the matter of opinions, ideas, literary manifestations, or merely of dress, how many persons are bold enough to run counter to the fashion? It is by examples not by arguments that crowds are guided. At every period there exists a small number of individualities which react upon the remainder and are imitated by the unconscious mass. It is needful however, that these individualities should not be in too pronounced disagreement with received ideas. Were they so, to imitate them would be too difficult and their influence would be nil. For this very reason men who are too superior to their epoch are generally without influence upon it. The line of separation is too strongly marked. For the same reason too Europeans, in spite of all the advantages of their civilisation, have so insignificant an influence on Eastern people; they differ from them to too great an extent.

"The dual action of the past and of reciprocal imitation renders, in the long run, all the men of the same country and the same period so alike that even in the case of individuals who would seem destined to escape this double influence, such as philosophers, learned men, and men of letters, thought and style have a family air which enables the age to which they belong to be immediately recognised. It is not necessary to talk for long with an individual to attain to a thorough knowledge of what he reads, of his habitual occupations, and of the surroundings amid which he lives."

Contagion is so powerful that it forces upon individuals not only certain opinions, but certain modes of feeling as well. Contagion is the cause of the contempt in which, at a given period, certain works are held—the example of "Tannhauser" may be cited—which, a few years later, for the same reason are admired by those who were foremost in criticising them.

The opinions and beliefs of crowds are specially propagated by contagion, but never by reasoning. The conceptions at present rife among the working classes have been acquired at the public-house as the result of affirmation, repetition, and contagion, and indeed the mode of creation of the beliefs of crowds of every age has scarcely been different. Renan justly institutes a comparison between the first founders of Christianity and "the socialist working men spreading their ideas from public-house to public-house"; while Voltaire had already observed in connection with the Christian religion that "for more than a hundred years it was only embraced by the vilest riff-raff."

It will be noted that in cases analogous to those I have just cited, contagion, after having been at work among the popular classes, has spread to the higher classes of society. This is what we see happening at the present day with regard to the socialist doctrines which are beginning to be held by those who will yet be their first victims. Contagion is so powerful a force that even the sentiment of personal interest disappears under its action.

This is the explanation of the fact that every opinion adopted by the populace always ends in implanting itself with great vigour in the highest social strata, however obvious be the absurdity of the triumphant opinion. This reaction of the lower upon the higher social classes is the more curious, owing to the circumstance that the beliefs of the crowd always have their origin to a greater or less extent in some higher idea, which has often remained without influence in the sphere in which it was evolved. Leaders and agitators, subjugated by this higher idea, take hold of it, distort it and create a sect which distorts it afresh, and then propagates it amongst the masses, who carry the process of deformation still further. Become a popular truth the idea returns, as it were, to its source and exerts an influence on the upper classes of a nation. In the long run it is intelligence that shapes the destiny of the world, but very indirectly. The philosophers who evolve ideas have long since returned to dust, when, as the result of the process I have just described, the fruit of their reflection ends by triumphing.

3. PRESTIGE

Great power is given to ideas propagated by affirmation, repetition, and contagion by the circumstance that they acquire in time that mysterious force known as prestige.

Whatever has been a ruling power in the world, whether it be ideas or men, has in the main enforced its authority by means of that irresistible force expressed by the word "prestige." The term is one whose meaning is grasped by everybody, but the word is employed in ways too different for it to be easy to define it. Prestige may involve such sentiments as admiration or fear. Occasionally even these sentiments are its basis, but it can perfectly well exist without them. The greatest measure of prestige is possessed by the dead, by beings, that is, of whom we do not stand in fear—by Alexander, Caesar, Mahomet, and Buddha, for example. On the other hand, there are fictive beings whom we do not admire—the monstrous divinities of the subterranean temples of India, for instance—but who strike us nevertheless as endowed with a great prestige.

Prestige in reality is a sort of domination exercised on our mind by an individual, a work, or an idea. This domination entirely paralyses our critical faculty, and fills our soul with astonishment and respect. The sentiment provoked is inexplicable, like all sentiments, but it would appear to be of the same kind as the fascination to which a magnetised person is subjected. Prestige is the mainspring of all authority. Neither gods, kings, nor women have ever reigned without it.

The various kinds of prestige may be grouped under two principal heads: acquired prestige and personal prestige. Acquired prestige is that resulting from name, fortune, and reputation. It may be independent of personal prestige. Personal prestige, on the contrary, is something essentially peculiar to the individual; it may coexist with reputation, glory, and fortune, or be strengthened by them, but it is perfectly capable of existing in their absence.

Acquired or artificial prestige is much the most common. The mere fact that an individual occupies a certain position, possesses a certain fortune, or bears certain titles, endows him with prestige, however slight his own personal worth. A soldier in uniform, a judge in his robes, always enjoys prestige. Pascal has very properly noted the necessity for judges of robes and wigs. Without them they would be stripped of half their authority. The most unbending socialist is always somewhat impressed by the sight of a prince or a marquis; and the assumption of such titles makes the robbing of tradesmen an easy matter.

"I had observed, under various circumstances, the peculiar sort of intoxication produced in the most reasonable Englishmen by the contact or sight of an English peer.

"Provided his fortune enables him to keep up his rank, he is sure of their affection in advance, and brought into contact with him they are so enchanted as to put up with anything at his hands. They may be seen to redden with pleasure at his approach, and if he speaks to them their suppressed joy increases their redness, and causes their eyes to gleam with unusual brilliance. Respect for nobility is in their blood, so to speak, as with Spaniards the love of dancing, with Germans that of music, and with Frenchmen the liking for revolutions. Their passion for horses and Shakespeare is less violent, the satisfaction and pride they derive from these sources a less integral part of their being. There is a considerable sale for books dealing with the peerage, and go where one will they are to be found, like the Bible, in all hands."

The prestige of which I have just spoken is exercised by persons; side by side with it may be placed that exercised by opinions, literary and artistic works, &c. Prestige of the latter kind is most often merely the result of accumulated repetitions. History, literary and artistic history especially, being nothing more than the repetition of identical judgments, which nobody endeavours to verify, every one ends by repeating what he learnt at school, till there come to be names and things which nobody would venture to meddle with. For a modern reader the perusal of Homer results incontestably in immense boredom; but who would venture to say so? The Parthenon, in its present state, is a wretched ruin, utterly destitute of interest, but it is endowed with such prestige that it does not appear to us as it really is, but with all its accompaniment of historic memories. The special characteristic of prestige is to prevent us seeing things as they are and to entirely paralyse our judgment. Crowds always, and individuals as a rule, stand in need of ready-made opinions on all subjects. The popularity of these opinions is independent of the measure of truth or error they contain, and is solely regulated by their prestige.

I now come to personal prestige. Its nature is very different from that of artificial or acquired prestige, with which I have just been concerned. It is a faculty independent of all titles, of all authority, and possessed by a small number of persons whom it enables to exercise a veritably magnetic fascination on those around them, although they are socially their equals, and lack all ordinary means of domination. They force the acceptance of their ideas and sentiments on those about them, and they are obeyed as is the tamer of wild beasts by the animal that could easily devour him.

The great leaders of crowds, such as Buddha, Jesus, Mahomet, Joan of Arc, and Napoleon, have possessed this form of prestige in a high degree, and to this endowment is more particularly due the position they attained. Gods, heroes, and dogmas win their way in the world of their own inward strength. They are not to be discussed: they disappear, indeed, as soon as discussed.

The great personages I have just cited were in possession of their power of fascination long before they became illustrious, and would never have become so without it. It is evident, for instance, that Napoleon at the zenith of his glory enjoyed an immense prestige by the mere fact of his power, but he was already endowed in part with this prestige when he was without power and completely unknown. When, an obscure general, he was sent, thanks to influential protection, to command the army of Italy, he found himself among rough generals who were of a mind to give a hostile reception to the young intruder dispatched them by the Directory. From the very beginning, from the first interview, without the aid of speeches, gestures, or threats, at the first sight of the man who was to become great they were vanquished. Taine furnishes a curious account of this interview taken from contemporary memoirs.

"The generals of division, amongst others Augereau, a sort of swashbuckler, uncouth and heroic, proud of his height and his bravery, arrive at the staff quarters very badly disposed towards the little upstart dispatched them from Paris. On the strength of the description of him that has been given them, Augereau is inclined to be insolent and insubordinate; a favourite of Barras, a general who owes his rank to the events of Vendemiaire who has won his grade by street-fighting, who is looked upon as bearish, because he is always thinking in solitude, of poor aspect, and with the reputation of a mathematician and dreamer. They are introduced, and Bonaparte keeps them waiting. At last he appears, girt with his sword; he puts on his hat, explains the measures he has taken, gives his orders, and dismisses them. Augereau has remained silent; it is only when he is outside that he regains his self-possession and is able to deliver himself of his customary oaths. He admits with Massena that this little devil of a general has inspired him with awe; he cannot understand the ascendency by which from the very first he has felt himself overwhelmed."

Become a great man, his prestige increased in proportion as his glory grew, and came to be at least equal to that of a divinity in the eyes of those devoted to him. General Vandamme, a rough, typical soldier of the Revolution, even more brutal and energetic than Augereau, said of him to Marshal d'Arnano in 1815, as on one occasion they mounted together the stairs of the Tuileries: "That devil of a man exercises a fascination on me that I cannot explain even to myself, and in such a degree that, though I fear neither God nor devil, when I am in his presence I am ready to tremble like a child, and he could make me go through the eye of a needle to throw myself into the fire."

Napoleon exercised a like fascination on all who came into contact with him.

Davoust used to say, talking of Maret's devotion and of his own: "Had the Emperor said to us, `It is important in the interest of my policy that Paris should be destroyed without a single person leaving it or escaping,' Maret I am sure would have kept the secret, but he could not have abstained from compromising himself by seeing that his family got clear of the city. On the other hand, I, for fear of letting the truth leak out, would have let my wife and children stay."

It is necessary to bear in mind the astounding power exerted by fascination of this order to understand that marvellous return from the Isle of Elba, that lightning-like conquest of France by an isolated man confronted by all the organised forces of a great country that might have been supposed weary of his tyranny. He had merely to cast a look at the generals sent to lay hands on him, and who had sworn to accomplish their mission. All of them submitted without discussion.

"Napoleon," writes the English General Wolseley, "lands in France almost alone, a fugitive from the small island of Elba which was his kingdom, and succeeded in a few weeks, without bloodshed, in upsetting all organised authority in France under its legitimate king; is it possible for the personal ascendency of a man to affirm itself in a more astonishing manner? But from the beginning to the end of this campaign, which was his last, how remarkable too is the ascendency he exercised over the Allies, obliging them to follow his initiative, and how near he came to crushing them!"

His prestige outlived him and continued to grow. It is his prestige that made an emperor of his obscure nephew. How powerful is his memory still is seen in the resurrection of his legend in progress at the present day. Ill-treat men as you will, massacre them by millions, be the cause of invasion upon invasion, all is permitted you if you possess prestige in a sufficient degree and the talent necessary to uphold it.

I have invoked, no doubt, in this case a quite exceptional example of prestige, but one it was useful to cite to make clear the genesis of great religions, great doctrines, and great empires. Were it not for the power exerted on the crowd by prestige, such growths would be incomprehensible.

Prestige, however, is not based solely on personal ascendency, military glory, and religious terror; it may have a more modest origin and still be considerable. Our century furnishes several examples. One of the most striking ones that posterity will recall from age to age will be supplied by the history of the illustrious man who modified the face of the globe and the commercial relations of the nations by separating two continents. He succeeded in his enterprise owing to his immense strength of will, but also owing to the fascination he exercised on those surrounding him. To overcome the unanimous opposition he met with, he had only to show himself. He would speak briefly, and in face of the charm he exerted his opponents became his friends. The English in particular strenuously opposed his scheme; he had only to put in an appearance in England to rally all suffrages. In later years, when he passed Southampton, the bells were rung on his passage; and at the present day a movement is on foot in England to raise a statue in his honour.

"Having vanquished whatever there is to vanquish, men and things, marshes, rocks, and sandy wastes," he had ceased to believe in obstacles, and wished to begin Suez over again at Panama. He began again with the same methods as of old; but he had aged, and, besides, the faith that moves mountains does not move them if they are too lofty. The mountains resisted, and the catastrophe that ensued destroyed the glittering aureole of glory that enveloped the hero. His life teaches how prestige can grow and how it can vanish. After rivalling in greatness the most famous heroes of history, he was lowered by the magistrates of his country to the ranks of the vilest criminals. When he died his coffin, unattended, traversed an indifferent crowd. Foreign sovereigns are alone in rendering homage to his memory as to that of one of the greatest men that history has known.

"After the condemnation of Ferdinand de Lesseps one has no longer the right to be astonished at the sad end of Christopher Columbus. If Ferdinand de Lesseps were a rogue every noble illusion is a crime. Antiquity would have crowned the memory of de Lesseps with an aureole of glory, and would have made him drink from the bowl of nectar in the midst of Olympus, for he has altered the face of the earth and accomplished works which make the creation more perfect. The President of the Court of Appeal has immortalised himself by condemning Ferdinand de Lesseps, for the nations will always demand the name of the man who was not afraid to debase his century by investing with the convict's cap an aged man, whose life redounded to the glory of his contemporaries.

"Let there be no more talk in the future of inflexible justice, there where reigns a bureaucratic hatred of audacious feats. The nations have need of audacious men who believe in themselves and overcome every obstacle without concern for their personal safety. Genius cannot be prudent; by dint of prudence it could never enlarge the sphere of human activity.

"... Ferdinand de Lesseps has known the intoxication of triumph and the bitterness of disappointment—Suez and Panama. At this point the heart revolts at the morality of success. When de Lesseps had succeeded in joining two seas princes and nations rendered him their homage; to-day, when he meets with failure among the rocks of the Cordilleras, he is nothing but a vulgar rogue.... In this result we see a war between the classes of society, the discontent of bureaucrats and employes, who take their revenge with the aid of the criminal code on those who would raise themselves above their fellows.... Modern legislators are filled with embarrassment when confronted by the lofty ideas due to human genius; the public comprehends such ideas still less, and it is easy for an advocate-general to prove that Stanley is a murderer and de Lesseps a deceiver."

Still, the various examples that have just been cited represent extreme cases. To fix in detail the psychology of prestige, it would be necessary to place them at the extremity of a series, which would range from the founders of religions and empires to the private individual who endeavours to dazzle his neighbours by a new coat or a decoration.

Between the extreme limits of this series would find a place all the forms of prestige resulting from the different elements composing a civilisation—sciences, arts, literature, &c.—and it would be seen that prestige constitutes the fundamental element of persuasion. Consciously or not, the being, the idea, or the thing possessing prestige is immediately imitated in consequence of contagion, and forces an entire generation to adopt certain modes of feeling and of giving expression to its thought. This imitation, moreover, is, as a rule, unconscious, which accounts for the fact that it is perfect. The modern painters who copy the pale colouring and the stiff attitudes of some of the Primitives are scarcely alive to the source of their inspiration. They believe in their own sincerity, whereas, if an eminent master had not revived this form of art, people would have continued blind to all but its naive and inferior sides. Those artists who, after the manner of another illustrious master, inundate their canvasses with violet shades do not see in nature more violet than was detected there fifty years ago; but they are influenced, "suggestioned," by the personal and special impressions of a painter who, in spite of this eccentricity, was successful in acquiring great prestige. Similar examples might be brought forward in connection with all the elements of civilisation.

It is seen from what precedes that a number of factors may be concerned in the genesis of prestige; among them success was always one of the most important. Every successful man, every idea that forces itself into recognition, ceases, ipso facto, to be called in question. The proof that success is one of the principal stepping-stones to prestige is that the disappearance of the one is almost always followed by the disappearance of the other. The hero whom the crowd acclaimed yesterday is insulted to-day should he have been overtaken by failure. The reaction, indeed, will be the stronger in proportion as the prestige has been great. The crowd in this case considers the fallen hero as an equal, and takes its revenge for having bowed to a superiority whose existence it no longer admits. While Robespierre was causing the execution of his colleagues and of a great number of his contemporaries, he possessed an immense prestige. When the transposition of a few votes deprived him of power, he immediately lost his prestige, and the crowd followed him to the guillotine with the self-same imprecations with which shortly before it had pursued his victims. Believers always break the statues of their former gods with every symptom of fury.

Prestige lost by want of success disappears in a brief space of time. It can also be worn away, but more slowly by being subjected to discussion. This latter power, however, is exceedingly sure. From the moment prestige is called in question it ceases to be prestige. The gods and men who have kept their prestige for long have never tolerated discussion. For the crowd to admire, it must be kept at a distance.

CHAPTER IV: LIMITATIONS OF THE VARIABILITY OF THE BELIEFS AND OPINIONS OF CROWDS

1. FIXED BELIEFS. The invariability of certain general beliefs—They shape the course of a civilisation—The difficulty of uprooting them—In what respect intolerance is a virtue in a people—The philosophic absurdity of a belief cannot interfere with its spreading. 2. THE CHANGEABLE OPINIONS OF CROWDS. The extreme mobility of opinions which do not arise from general beliefs—Apparent variations of ideas and beliefs in less than a century—The real limits of these variations—The matters effected by the variation—The disappearance at present in progress of general beliefs, and the extreme diffusion of the newspaper press, have for result that opinions are nowadays more and more changeable—Why the opinions of crowds tend on the majority of subjects towards indifference—Governments now powerless to direct opinion as they formerly did—Opinions prevented to-day from being tyrannical on account of their exceeding divergency.

1. FIXED BELIEFS

A close parallel exists between the anatomical and psychological characteristics of living beings. In these anatomical characteristics certain invariable, or slightly variable, elements are met with, to change which the lapse is necessary of geological ages. Side by side with these fixed, indestructible features are to be found others extremely changeable, which the art of the breeder or horticulturist may easily modify, and at times to such an extent as to conceal the fundamental characteristics from an observer at all inattentive.

The same phenomenon is observed in the case of moral characteristics. Alongside the unalterable psychological elements of a race, mobile and changeable elements are to be encountered. For this reason, in studying the beliefs and opinions of a people, the presence is always detected of a fixed groundwork on which are engrafted opinions as changing as the surface sand on a rock.

The opinions and beliefs of crowds may be divided, then, into two very distinct classes. On the one hand we have great permanent beliefs, which endure for several centuries, and on which an entire civilisation may rest. Such, for instance, in the past were feudalism, Christianity, and Protestantism; and such, in our own time, are the nationalist principle and contemporary democratic and social ideas. In the second place, there are the transitory, changing opinions, the outcome, as a rule, of general conceptions, of which every age sees the birth and disappearance; examples in point are the theories which mould literature and the arts—those, for instance, which produced romanticism, naturalism, mysticism, &c. Opinions of this order are as superficial, as a rule, as fashion, and as changeable. They may be compared to the ripples which ceaselessly arise and vanish on the surface of a deep lake.

The great generalised beliefs are very restricted in number. Their rise and fall form the culminating points of the history of every historic race. They constitute the real framework of civilisation.

It is easy to imbue the mind of crowds with a passing opinion, but very difficult to implant therein a lasting belief. However, a belief of this latter description once established, it is equally difficult to uproot it. It is usually only to be changed at the cost of violent revolutions. Even revolutions can only avail when the belief has almost entirely lost its sway over men's minds. In that case revolutions serve to finally sweep away what had already been almost cast aside, though the force of habit prevented its complete abandonment. The beginning of a revolution is in reality the end of a belief.

The precise moment at which a great belief is doomed is easily recognisable; it is the moment when its value begins to be called in question. Every general belief being little else than a fiction, it can only survive on the condition that it be not subjected to examination.

But even when a belief is severely shaken, the institutions to which it has given rise retain their strength and disappear but slowly. Finally, when the belief has completely lost its force, all that rested upon it is soon involved in ruin. As yet a nation has never been able to change its beliefs without being condemned at the same time to transform all the elements of its civilisation. The nation continues this process of transformation until it has alighted on and accepted a new general belief: until this juncture it is perforce in a state of anarchy. General beliefs are the indispensable pillars of civilisations; they determine the trend of ideas. They alone are capable of inspiring faith and creating a sense of duty.

Nations have always been conscious of the utility of acquiring general beliefs, and have instinctively understood that their disappearance would be the signal for their own decline. In the case of the Romans, the fanatical cult of Rome was the belief that made them masters of the world, and when the belief had died out Rome was doomed to die. As for the barbarians who destroyed the Roman civilisation, it was only when they had acquired certain commonly accepted beliefs that they attained a measure of cohesion and emerged from anarchy.

Plainly it is not for nothing that nations have always displayed intolerance in the defence of their opinions. This intolerance, open as it is to criticism from the philosophic standpoint, represents in the life of a people the most necessary of virtues. It was to found or uphold general beliefs that so many victims were sent to the stake in the Middle Ages and that so many inventors and innovators have died in despair even if they have escaped martyrdom. It is in defence, too, of such beliefs that the world has been so often the scene of the direst disorder, and that so many millions of men have died on the battlefield, and will yet die there.

There are great difficulties in the way of establishing a general belief, but when it is definitely implanted its power is for a long time to come invincible, and however false it be philosophically it imposes itself upon the most luminous intelligence. Have not the European peoples regarded as incontrovertible for more than fifteen centuries religious legends which, closely examined, are as barbarous as those of Moloch? The frightful absurdity of the legend of a God who revenges himself for the disobedience of one of his creatures by inflicting horrible tortures on his son remained unperceived during many centuries. Such potent geniuses as a Galileo, a Newton, and a Leibnitz never supposed for an instant that the truth of such dogmas could be called in question. Nothing can be more typical than this fact of the hypnotising effect of general beliefs, but at the same time nothing can mark more decisively the humiliating limitations of our intelligence.

As soon as a new dogma is implanted in the mind of crowds it becomes the source of inspiration whence are evolved its institutions, arts, and mode of existence. The sway it exerts over men's minds under these circumstances is absolute. Men of action have no thought beyond realising the accepted belief, legislators beyond applying it, while philosophers, artists, and men of letters are solely preoccupied with its expression under various shapes.

From the fundamental belief transient accessory ideas may arise, but they always bear the impress of the belief from which they have sprung. The Egyptian civilisation, the European civilisation of the Middle Ages, the Mussulman civilisation of the Arabs are all the outcome of a small number of religious beliefs which have left their mark on the least important elements of these civilisations and allow of their immediate recognition.

Thus it is that, thanks to general beliefs, the men of every age are enveloped in a network of traditions, opinions, and customs which render them all alike, and from whose yoke they cannot extricate themselves. Men are guided in their conduct above all by their beliefs and by the customs that are the consequence of those beliefs. These beliefs and customs regulate the smallest acts of our existence, and the most independent spirit cannot escape their influence. The tyranny exercised unconsciously on men's minds is the only real tyranny, because it cannot be fought against. Tiberius, Ghengis Khan, and Napoleon were assuredly redoubtable tyrants, but from the depth of their graves Moses, Buddha, Jesus, and Mahomet have exerted on the human soul a far profounder despotism. A conspiracy may overthrow a tyrant, but what can it avail against a firmly established belief? In its violent struggle with Roman Catholicism it is the French Revolution that has been vanquished, and this in spite of the fact that the sympathy of the crowd was apparently on its side, and in spite of recourse to destructive measures as pitiless as those of the Inquisition. The only real tyrants that humanity has known have always been the memories of its dead or the illusions it has forged itself.

The philosophic absurdity that often marks general beliefs has never been an obstacle to their triumph. Indeed the triumph of such beliefs would seem impossible unless on the condition that they offer some mysterious absurdity. In consequence, the evident weakness of the socialist beliefs of to-day will not prevent them triumphing among the masses. Their real inferiority to all religious beliefs is solely the result of this consideration, that the ideal of happiness offered by the latter being realisable only in a future life, it was beyond the power of anybody to contest it. The socialist ideal of happiness being intended to be realised on earth, the vanity of its promises will at once appear as soon as the first efforts towards their realisation are made, and simultaneously the new belief will entirely lose its prestige. Its strength, in consequence, will only increase until the day when, having triumphed, its practical realisation shall commence. For this reason, while the new religion exerts to begin with, like all those that have preceded it, a destructive influence, it will be unable, in the future, to play a creative part.

2. THE CHANGEABLE OPINIONS OF CROWDS

Above the substratum of fixed beliefs, whose power we have just demonstrated, is found an overlying growth of opinions, ideas, and thoughts which are incessantly springing up and dying out. Some of them exist but for a day, and the more important scarcely outlive a generation. We have already noted that the changes which supervene in opinions of this order are at times far more superficial than real, and that they are always affected by racial considerations. When examining, for instance, the political institutions of France we showed that parties to all appearance utterly distinct—royalists, radicals, imperialists, socialists, &c.—have an ideal absolutely identical, and that this ideal is solely dependent on the mental structure of the French race, since a quite contrary ideal is found under analogous names among other races. Neither the name given to opinions nor deceptive adaptations alter the essence of things. The men of the Great Revolution, saturated with Latin literature, who (their eyes fixed on the Roman Republic), adopted its laws, its fasces, and its togas, did not become Romans because they were under the empire of a powerful historical suggestion. The task of the philosopher is to investigate what it is which subsists of ancient beliefs beneath their apparent changes, and to identify amid the moving flux of opinions the part determined by general beliefs and the genius of the race.

In the absence of this philosophic test it might be supposed that crowds change their political or religious beliefs frequently and at will. All history, whether political, religious, artistic, or literary, seems to prove that such is the case.

As an example, let us take a very short period of French history, merely that from 1790 to 1820, a period of thirty years' duration, that of a generation. In the course of it we see the crowd at first monarchical become very revolutionary, then very imperialist, and again very monarchical. In the matter of religion it gravitates in the same lapse of time from Catholicism to atheism, then towards deism, and then returns to the most pronounced forms of Catholicism. These changes take place not only amongst the masses, but also amongst those who direct them. We observe with astonishment the prominent men of the Convention, the sworn enemies of kings, men who would have neither gods nor masters, become the humble servants of Napoleon, and afterwards, under Louis XVIII., piously carry candles in religious processions.

Numerous, too, are the changes in the opinions of the crowd in the course of the following seventy years. The "Perfidious Albion" of the opening of the century is the ally of France under Napoleon's heir; Russia, twice invaded by France, which looked on with satisfaction at French reverses, becomes its friend.

In literature, art, and philosophy the successive evolutions of opinion are more rapid still. Romanticism, naturalism, mysticism, &c., spring up and die out in turn. The artist and the writer applauded yesterday are treated on the morrow with profound contempt.

When, however, we analyse all these changes in appearance so far reaching, what do we find? All those that are in opposition with the general beliefs and sentiments of the race are of transient duration, and the diverted stream soon resumes its course. The opinions which are not linked to any general belief or sentiment of the race, and which in consequence cannot possess stability, are at the mercy of every chance, or, if the expression be preferred, of every change in the surrounding circumstances. Formed by suggestion and contagion, they are always momentary; they crop up and disappear as rapidly on occasion as the sandhills formed by the wind on the sea-coast.

At the present day the changeable opinions of crowds are greater in number than they ever were, and for three different reasons.

The first is that as the old beliefs are losing their influence to a greater and greater extent, they are ceasing to shape the ephemeral opinions of the moment as they did in the past. The weakening of general beliefs clears the ground for a crop of haphazard opinions without a past or a future.

The second reason is that the power of crowds being on the increase, and this power being less and less counterbalanced, the extreme mobility of ideas, which we have seen to be a peculiarity of crowds, can manifest itself without let or hindrance.

Finally, the third reason is the recent development of the newspaper press, by whose agency the most contrary opinions are being continually brought before the attention of crowds. The suggestions that might result from each individual opinion are soon destroyed by suggestions of an opposite character. The consequence is that no opinion succeeds in becoming widespread, and that the existence of all of them is ephemeral. An opinion nowadays dies out before it has found a sufficiently wide acceptance to become general.

A phenomenon quite new in the world's history, and most characteristic of the present age, has resulted from these different causes; I allude to the powerlessness of governments to direct opinion.

In the past, and in no very distant past, the action of governments and the influence of a few writers and a very small number of newspapers constituted the real reflectors of public opinion. To-day the writers have lost all influence, and the newspapers only reflect opinion. As for statesmen, far from directing opinion, their only endeavour is to follow it. They have a dread of opinion, which amounts at times to terror, and causes them to adopt an utterly unstable line of conduct.

The opinion of crowds tends, then, more and more to become the supreme guiding principle in politics. It goes so far to-day as to force on alliances, as has been seen recently in the case of the Franco-Russian alliance, which is solely the outcome of a popular movement. A curious symptom of the present time is to observe popes, kings, and emperors consent to be interviewed as a means of submitting their views on a given subject to the judgment of crowds. Formerly it might have been correct to say that politics were not a matter of sentiment. Can the same be said to-day, when politics are more and more swayed by the impulse of changeable crowds, who are uninfluenced by reason and can only be guided by sentiment?

As to the press, which formerly directed opinion, it has had, like governments, to humble itself before the power of crowds. It wields, no doubt, a considerable influence, but only because it is exclusively the reflection of the opinions of crowds and of their incessant variations. Become a mere agency for the supply of information, the press has renounced all endeavour to enforce an idea or a doctrine. It follows all the changes of public thought, obliged to do so by the necessities of competition under pain of losing its readers. The old staid and influential organs of the past, such as the

Constitutionnel, the Debats, or the Siecle, which were accepted as oracles by the preceding generation, have disappeared or have become typical modern papers, in which a maximum of news is sandwiched in between light articles, society gossip, and financial puffs. There can be no question to-day of a paper rich enough to allow its contributors to air their personal opinions, and such opinions would be of slight weight with readers who only ask to be kept informed or to be amused, and who suspect every affirmation of being prompted by motives of speculation. Even the critics have ceased to be able to assure the success of a book or a play. They are capable of doing harm, but not of doing a service. The papers are so conscious of the uselessness of everything in the shape of criticism or personal opinion, that they have reached the point of suppressing literary criticism, confining themselves to citing the title of a book, and appending a "puff" of two or three lines. In twenty years' time the same fate will probably have overtaken theatrical criticism.

The close watching of the course of opinion has become to-day the principal preoccupation of the press and of governments. The effect produced by an event, a legislative proposal, a speech, is without intermission what they require to know, and the task is not easy, for nothing is more mobile and changeable than the thought of crowds, and nothing more frequent than to see them execrate to-day what they applauded yesterday.

This total absence of any sort of direction of opinion, and at the same time the destruction of general beliefs, have had for final result an extreme divergency of convictions of every order, and a growing indifference on the part of crowds to everything that does not plainly touch their immediate interests. Questions of doctrine, such as socialism, only recruit champions boasting genuine convictions among the quite illiterate classes, among the workers in mines and factories, for instance. Members of the lower middle class, and working men possessing some degree of instruction, have either become utterly sceptical or extremely unstable in their opinions.

The evolution which has been effected in this direction in the last twenty-five years is striking. During the preceding period, comparatively near us though it is, opinions still had a certain general trend; they had their origin in the acceptance of some fundamental belief. By the mere fact that an individual was a monarchist he possessed inevitably certain clearly defined ideas in history as well as in science, while by the mere fact that he was a republican, his ideas were quite contrary. A monarchist was well aware that men are not descended from monkeys, and a republican was not less well aware that such is in truth their descent. It was the duty of the monarchist to speak with horror, and of the republican to speak with veneration, of the great Revolution. There were certain names, such as those of Robespierre and Marat, that had to be uttered with an air of religious devotion, and other names, such as those of Caesar, Augustus, or Napoleon, that ought never to be mentioned unaccompanied by a torrent of invective. Even in the French Sorbonne this ingenuous fashion of conceiving history was general.

"The taking of the Bastille was a culminating event in the history not only of France, but of all Europe; and inaugurated a new epoch in the history of the world!"

With respect to Robespierre, we learn with stupefaction that "his dictatorship was based more especially on opinion, persuasion, and moral authority; it was a sort of pontificate in the hands of a virtuous man!" (pp. 91 and 220.)

At the present day, as the result of discussion and analysis, all opinions are losing their prestige; their distinctive features are rapidly worn away, and few survive capable of arousing our enthusiasm. The man of modern times is more and more a prey to indifference.

The general wearing away of opinions should not be too greatly deplored. That it is a symptom of decadence in the life of a people cannot be contested. It is certain that men of immense, of almost supernatural insight, that apostles, leaders of crowds—men, in a word, of genuine and strong convictions—exert a far greater force than men who deny, who criticise, or who are indifferent, but it must not be forgotten that, given the power possessed at present by crowds, were a single opinion to acquire sufficient prestige to enforce its general acceptance, it would soon be endowed with so tyrannical a strength that everything would have to bend before it, and the era of free discussion would be closed for a long time. Crowds are occasionally easy-going masters, as were Heliogabalus and Tiberius, but they are also violently capricious. A civilisation, when the moment has come for crowds to acquire a high hand over it, is at the mercy of too many chances to endure for long. Could anything postpone for a while the hour of its ruin, it would be precisely the extreme instability of the opinions of crowds and their growing indifference with respect to all general beliefs.

BOOK III: THE CLASSIFICATION AND DESCRIPTION OF THE DIFFERENT KINDS OF CROWDS

CHAPTER I: THE CLASSIFICATION OF CROWDS

The general divisions of crowds—Their classification. 1. HETEROGENEOUS CROWDS. Different varieties of them—The influence of race—The spirit of the crowd is weak in proportion as the spirit of the race is strong—The spirit of the race represents the civilised state and the spirit of the crowd the barbarian state. 2. HOMOGENEOUS CROWDS. Their different varieties—Sects, castes, and classes.

We have sketched in this work the general characteristics common to psychological crowds. It remains to point out the particular characteristics which accompany those of a general order in the different categories of collectivities, when they are transformed into a crowd under the influences of the proper exciting causes. We will, first of all, set forth in a few words a classification of crowds.

Our starting-point will be the simple multitude. Its most inferior form is met with when the multitude is composed of individuals belonging to different races. In this case its only common bond of union is the will, more or less respected of a chief. The barbarians of very diverse origin who during several centuries invaded the Roman Empire, may be cited as a specimen of multitudes of this kind.

On a higher level than these multitudes composed of different races are those which under certain influences have acquired common characteristics, and have ended by forming a single race. They present at times characteristics peculiar to crowds, but these characteristics are overruled to a greater or less extent by racial considerations.

These two kinds of multitudes may, under certain influences investigated in this work, be transformed into organised or psychological crowds. We shall break up these organised crowds into the following divisions:—

1. Anonymous crowds (street
crowds, for example).
A. Heterogeneous 2. Crowds not anonymous
crowds. (juries, parliamentary assemblies,
&c.).
1. Sects (political sects,
religious sects, &c.).
2. Castes (the military caste,
B. Homogeneous the priestly caste, the
crowds. working caste, &c.).
3. Classes (the middle classes,
the peasant classes, &c.).

We will point out briefly the distinguishing characteristics of these different categories of crowds.

1. HETEROGENEOUS CROWDS

It is these collectivities whose characteristics have been studied in this volume. They are composed of individuals of any description, of any profession, and any degree of intelligence.

We are now aware that by the mere fact that men form part of a crowd engaged in action, their collective psychology differs essentially from their individual psychology, and their intelligence is affected by this differentiation. We have seen that intelligence is without influence in collectivities, they being solely under the sway of unconscious sentiments.

A fundamental factor, that of race, allows of a tolerably thorough differentiation of the various heterogeneous crowds.

We have often referred already to the part played by race, and have shown it to be the most powerful of the factors capable of determining men's actions. Its action is also to be traced in the character of crowds. A crowd composed of individuals assembled at haphazard, but all of them Englishmen or Chinamen, will differ widely from another crowd also composed of individuals of any and every description, but of other races—Russians, Frenchmen, or Spaniards, for example.

The wide divergencies which their inherited mental constitution creates in men's modes of feeling and thinking at once come into prominence when, which rarely happens, circumstances gather together in the same crowd and in fairly equal proportions individuals of different nationality, and this occurs, however identical in appearance be the interests which provoked the gathering. The efforts made by the socialists to assemble in great congresses the representatives of the working-class populations of different countries, have always ended in the most pronounced discord. A Latin crowd, however revolutionary or however conservative it be supposed, will invariably appeal to the intervention of the State to realise its demands. It is always distinguished by a marked tendency towards centralisation and by a leaning, more or less pronounced, in favour of a dictatorship. An English or an American crowd, on the contrary, sets no store on the State, and only appeals to private initiative. A French crowd lays particular weight on equality and an English crowd on liberty. These differences of race explain how it is that there are almost as many different forms of socialism and democracy as there are nations.

The genius of the race, then, exerts a paramount influence upon the dispositions of a crowd. It is the powerful underlying force that limits its changes of humour. It should be considered as an essential law that THE INFERIOR CHARACTERISTICS OF CROWDS ARE THE LESS ACCENTUATED IN PROPORTION AS THE SPIRIT OF THE RACE IS STRONG. The crowd state and the domination of crowds is equivalent to the barbarian state, or to a return to it. It is by the acquisition of a solidly constituted collective spirit that the race frees itself to a greater and greater extent from the unreflecting power of crowds, and emerges from the barbarian state. The only important classification to be made of heterogeneous crowds, apart from that based on racial considerations, is to separate them into anonymous crowds, such as street crowds, and crowds not anonymous—deliberative assemblies and juries, for example. The sentiment of responsibility absent from crowds of the first description and developed in those of the second often gives a very different tendency to their respective acts.

2. HOMOGENEOUS CROWDS

Homogeneous crowds include: 1. Sects; 2. Castes; 3. Classes.

The SECT represents the first step in the process of organisation of homogeneous crowds. A sect includes individuals differing greatly as to their education, their professions, and the class of society to which they belong, and with their common beliefs as the connecting link. Examples in point are religious and political sects.

The CASTE represents the highest degree of organisation of which the crowd is susceptible. While the sect includes individuals of very different professions, degrees of education and social surrounding, who are only linked together by the beliefs they hold in common, the caste is composed of individuals of the same profession, and in consequence similarly educated and of much the same social status. Examples in point are the military and priestly castes.

The CLASS is formed of individuals of diverse origin, linked together not by a community of beliefs, as are the members of a sect, or by common professional occupations, as are the members of a caste, but by certain interests and certain habits of life and education almost identical. The middle class and the agricultural class are examples.

Being only concerned in this work with heterogeneous crowds, and reserving the study of homogeneous crowds (sects, castes, and classes) for another volume, I shall not insist here on the characteristics of crowds of this latter kind. I shall conclude this study of heterogeneous crowds by the examination of a few typical and distinct categories of crowds.

CHAPTER II: CROWDS TERMED CRIMINAL CROWDS

Crowds termed criminal crowds—A crowd may be legally yet not psychologically criminal—The absolute unconsciousness of the acts of crowds—Various examples—Psychology of the authors of the September massacres—Their reasoning, their sensibility, their ferocity, and their morality.

Owing to the fact that crowds, after a period of excitement, enter upon a purely automatic and unconscious state, in which they are guided by suggestion, it seems difficult to qualify them in any case as criminal. I only retain this erroneous qualification because it has been definitely brought into vogue by recent psychological investigations. Certain acts of crowds are assuredly criminal, if considered merely in themselves, but criminal in that case in the same way as the act of a tiger devouring a Hindoo, after allowing its young to maul him for their amusement.

The usual motive of the crimes of crowds is a powerful suggestion, and the individuals who take part in such crimes are afterwards convinced that they have acted in obedience to duty, which is far from being the case with the ordinary criminal.

The history of the crimes committed by crowds illustrates what precedes.

The murder of M. de Launay, the governor of the Bastille, may be cited as a typical example. After the taking of the fortress the governor, surrounded by a very excited crowd, was dealt blows from every direction. It was proposed to hang him, to cut off his head, to tie him to a horse's tail. While struggling, he accidently kicked one of those present. Some one proposed, and his suggestion was at once received with acclamation by the crowd, that the individual who had been kicked should cut the governor's throat.

"The individual in question, a cook out of work, whose chief reason for being at the Bastille was idle curiosity as to what was going on, esteems, that since such is the general opinion, the action is patriotic and even believes he deserves a medal for having destroyed a monster. With a sword that is lent him he strikes the bared neck, but the weapon being somewhat blunt and not cutting, he takes from his pocket a small black-handled knife and (in his capacity of cook he would be experienced in cutting up meat) successfully effects the operation."

The working of the process indicated above is clearly seen in this example. We have obedience to a suggestion, which is all the stronger because of its collective origin, and the murderer's conviction that he has committed a very meritorious act, a conviction the more natural seeing that he enjoys the unanimous approval of his fellow-citizens. An act of this kind may be considered crime legally but not psychologically.

The general characteristics of criminal crowds are precisely the same as those we have met with in all crowds: openness to suggestion, credulity, mobility, the exaggeration of the sentiments good or bad, the manifestation of certain forms of morality, &c.

We shall find all these characteristics present in a crowd which has left behind it in French history the most sinister memories—the crowd which perpetrated the September massacres. In point of fact it offers much similarity with the crowd that committed the Saint Bartholomew massacres. I borrow the details from the narration of M. Taine, who took them from contemporary sources.

It is not known exactly who gave the order or made the suggestion to empty the prisons by massacring the prisoners. Whether it was Danton, as is probable, or another does not matter; the one interesting fact for us is the powerful suggestion received by the crowd charged with the massacre.

The crowd of murderers numbered some three hundred persons, and was a perfectly typical heterogeneous crowd. With the exception of a very small number of professional scoundrels, it was composed in the main of shopkeepers and artisans of every trade: bootmakers, locksmiths, hairdressers, masons, clerks, messengers, &c. Under the influence of the suggestion received they are perfectly convinced, as was the cook referred to above, that they are accomplishing a patriotic duty. They fill a double office, being at once judge and executioner, but they do not for a moment regard themselves as criminals.

Deeply conscious of the importance of their duty, they begin by forming a sort of tribunal, and in connection with this act the ingenuousness of crowds and their rudimentary conception of justice are seen immediately. In consideration of the large number of the accused, it is decided that, to begin with, the nobles, priests, officers, and members of the king's household—in a word, all the individuals whose mere profession is proof of their guilt in the eyes of a good patriot—shall be slaughtered in a body, there being no need for a special decision in their case. The remainder shall be judged on their personal appearance and their reputation. In this way the rudimentary conscience of the crowd is satisfied. It will now be able to proceed legally with the massacre, and to give free scope to those instincts of ferocity whose genesis I have set forth elsewhere, they being instincts which collectivities always have it in them to develop to a high degree. These instincts, however—as is regularly the case in crowds—will not prevent the manifestation of other and contrary sentiments, such as a tenderheartedness often as extreme as the ferocity.

"They have the expansive sympathy and prompt sensibility of the Parisian working man. At the Abbaye, one of the federates, learning that the prisoners had been left without water for twenty-six hours, was bent on putting the gaoler to death, and would have done so but for the prayers of the prisoners themselves. When a prisoner is acquitted (by the improvised tribunal) every one, guards and slaughterers included, embraces him with transports of joy and applauds frantically," after which the wholesale massacre is recommenced. During its progress a pleasant gaiety never ceases to reign. There is dancing and singing around the corpses, and benches are arranged "for the ladies," delighted to witness the killing of aristocrats. The exhibition continues, moreover, of a special description of justice.

A slaughterer at the Abbaye having complained that the ladies placed at a little distance saw badly, and that only a few of those present had the pleasure of striking the aristocrats, the justice of the observation is admitted, and it is decided that the victims shall be made to pass slowly between two rows of slaughterers, who shall be under the obligation to strike with the back of the sword only so as to prolong the agony. At the prison de la Force the victims are stripped stark naked and literally "carved" for half an hour, after which, when every one has had a good view, they are finished off by a blow that lays bare their entrails.

The slaughterers, too, have their scruples and exhibit that moral sense whose existence in crowds we have already pointed out. They refuse to appropriate the money and jewels of the victims, taking them to the table of the committees.

Those rudimentary forms of reasoning, characteristic of the mind of crowds, are always to be traced in all their acts. Thus, after the slaughter of the 1,200 or 1,500 enemies of the nation, some one makes the remark, and his suggestion is at once adopted, that the other prisons, those containing aged beggars, vagabonds, and young prisoners, hold in reality useless mouths, of which it would be well on that account to get rid. Besides, among them there should certainly be enemies of the people, a woman of the name of Delarue, for instance, the widow of a poisoner: "She must be furious at being in prison, if she could she would set fire to Paris: she must have said so, she has said so. Another good riddance." The demonstration appears convincing, and the prisoners are massacred without exception, included in the number being some fifty children of from twelve to seventeen years of age, who, of course, might themselves have become enemies of the nation, and of whom in consequence it was clearly well to be rid.

At the end of a week's work, all these operations being brought to an end, the slaughterers can think of reposing themselves. Profoundly convinced that they have deserved well of their country, they went to the authorities and demanded a recompense. The most zealous went so far as to claim a medal.

The history of the Commune of 1871 affords several facts analogous to those which precede. Given the growing influence of crowds and the successive capitulations before them of those in authority, we are destined to witness many others of a like nature.

CHAPTER III: CRIMINAL JURIES

Criminal juries—General characteristics of juries—statistics show that their decisions are independent of their composition—The manner in which an impression may be made on juries—The style and influence of argument—The methods of persuasion of celebrated counsel—The nature of those crimes for which juries are respectively indulgent or severe—The utility of the jury as an institution, and the danger that would result from its place being taken by magistrates.

Being unable to study here every category of jury, I shall only examine the most important—that of the juries of the Court of Assize. These juries afford an excellent example of the heterogeneous crowd that is not anonymous. We shall find them display suggestibility and but slight capacity for reasoning, while they are open to the influence of the leaders of crowds, and they are guided in the main by unconscious sentiments. In the course of this investigation we shall have occasion to observe some interesting examples of the errors that may be made by persons not versed in the psychology of crowds.

Juries, in the first place, furnish us a good example of the slight importance of the mental level of the different elements composing a crowd, so far as the decisions it comes to are concerned. We have seen that when a deliberative assembly is called upon to give its opinion on a question of a character not entirely technical, intelligence stands for nothing. For instance, a gathering of scientific men or of artists, owing to the mere fact that they form an assemblage, will not deliver judgments on general subjects sensibly different from those rendered by a gathering of masons or grocers. At various periods, and in particular previous to 1848, the French administration instituted a careful choice among the persons summoned to form a jury, picking the jurors from among the enlightened classes; choosing professors, functionaries, men of letters, &c. At the present day jurors are recruited for the most part from among small tradesmen, petty capitalists, and employes. Yet, to the great astonishment of specialist writers, whatever the composition of the jury has been, its decisions have been identical. Even the magistrates, hostile as they are to the institution of the jury, have had to recognise the exactness of the assertion. M. Berard des Glajeux, a former President of the Court of Assizes, expresses himself on the subject in his "Memoirs" in the following terms:—

"The selection of jurymen is to-day in reality in the hands of the municipal councillors, who put people down on the list or eliminate them from it in accordance with the political and electoral preoccupations inherent in their situation.... The majority of the jurors chosen are persons engaged in trade, but persons of less importance than formerly, and employes belonging to certain branches of the administration.... Both opinions and professions counting for nothing once the role of judge assumed, many of the jurymen having the ardour of neophytes, and men of the best intentions being similarly disposed in humble situations, the spirit of the jury has not changed: ITS VERDICTS HAVE REMAINED THE SAME."

Of the passage just cited the conclusions, which are just, are to be borne in mind and not the explanations, which are weak. Too much astonishment should not be felt at this weakness, for, as a rule, counsel equally with magistrates seem to be ignorant of the psychology of crowds and, in consequence, of juries. I find a proof of this statement in a fact related by the author just quoted. He remarks that Lachaud, one of the most illustrious barristers practising in the Court of Assize, made systematic use of his right to object to a juror in the case of all individuals of intelligence on the list. Yet experience—and experience alone—has ended by acquainting us with the utter uselessness of these objections. This is proved by the fact that at the present day public prosecutors and barristers, at any rate those belonging to the Parisian bar, have entirely renounced their right to object to a juror; still, as M. des Glajeux remarks, the verdicts have not changed, "they are neither better nor worse."

Like all crowds, juries are very strongly impressed by sentimental considerations, and very slightly by argument. "They cannot resist the sight," writes a barrister, "of a mother giving its child the breast, or of orphans." "It is sufficient that a woman should be of agreeable appearance," says M. des Glajeux, "to win the benevolence of the jury."

Without pity for crimes of which it appears possible they might themselves be the victims—such crimes, moreover, are the most dangerous for society—juries, on the contrary, are very indulgent in the case of breaches of the law whose motive is passion. They are rarely severe on infanticide by girl-mothers, or hard on the young woman who throws vitriol at the man who has seduced and deserted her, for the reason that they feel instinctively that society runs but slight danger from such crimes, and that in a country in which the law does not protect deserted girls the crime of the girl who avenges herself is rather useful than harmful, inasmuch as it frightens future seducers in advance.

Juries, like all crowds, are profoundly impressed by prestige, and President des Glajeux very properly remarks that, very democratic as juries are in their composition, they are very aristocratic in their likes and dislikes: "Name, birth, great wealth, celebrity, the assistance of an illustrious counsel, everything in the nature of distinction or that lends brilliancy to the accused, stands him in extremely good stead."

The chief concern of a good counsel should be to work upon the feelings of the jury, and, as with all crowds, to argue but little, or only to employ rudimentary modes of reasoning. An English barrister, famous for his successes in the assize courts, has well set forth the line of action to be followed:—

"While pleading he would attentively observe the jury. The most favourable opportunity has been reached. By dint of insight and experience the counsel reads the effect of each phrase on the faces of the jurymen, and draws his conclusions in consequence. His first step is to be sure which members of the jury are already favourable to his cause. It is short work to definitely gain their adhesion, and having done so he turns his attention to the members who seem, on the contrary, ill-disposed, and endeavours to discover why they are hostile to the accused. This is the delicate part of his task, for there may be an infinity of reasons for condemning a man, apart from the sentiment of justice."

These few lines resume the entire mechanism of the art of oratory, and we see why the speech prepared in advance has so slight an effect, it being necessary to be able to modify the terms employed from moment to moment in accordance with the impression produced.

The orator does not require to convert to his views all the members of a jury, but only the leading spirits among it who will determine the general opinion. As in all crowds, so in juries there are a small number of individuals who serve as guides to the rest. "I have found by experience," says the counsel cited above, "that one or two energetic men suffice to carry the rest of the jury with them." It is those two or three whom it is necessary to convince by skilful suggestions. First of all, and above all, it is necessary to please them. The man forming part of a crowd whom one has succeeded in pleasing is on the point of being convinced, and is quite disposed to accept as excellent any arguments that may be offered him. I detach the following anecdote from an interesting account of M. Lachaud, alluded to above:—

"It is well known that during all the speeches he would deliver in the course of an assize sessions, Lachaud never lost sight of the two or three jurymen whom he knew or felt to be influential but obstinate. As a rule he was successful in winning over these refractory jurors. On one occasion, however, in the provinces, he had to deal with a juryman whom he plied in vain for three-quarters of an hour with his most cunning arguments; the man was the seventh juryman, the first on the second bench. The case was desperate. Suddenly, in the middle of a passionate demonstration, Lachaud stopped short, and addressing the President of the court said: `Would you give instructions for the curtain there in front to be drawn? The seventh juryman is blinded by the sun.' The juryman in question reddened, smiled, and expressed his thanks. He was won over for the defence."

Many writers, some of them most distinguished, have started of late a strong campaign against the institution of the jury, although it is the only protection we have against the errors, really very frequent, of a caste that is under no control. A portion of these writers advocate a jury recruited solely from the ranks of the enlightened classes; but we have already proved that even in this case the verdicts would be identical with those returned under the present system. Other writers, taking their stand on the errors committed by juries, would abolish the jury and replace it by judges. It is difficult to see how these would-be reformers can forget that the errors for which the jury is blamed were committed in the first instance by judges, and that when the accused person comes before a jury he has already been held to be guilty by several magistrates, by the juge d'instruction, the public prosecutor, and the Court of Arraignment. It should thus be clear that were the accused to be definitely judged by magistrates instead of by jurymen, he would lose his only chance of being admitted innocent. The errors of juries have always been first of all the errors of magistrates. It is solely the magistrates, then, who should be blamed when particularly monstrous judicial errors crop up, such, for instance, as the quite recent condemnation of Dr. L—— who, prosecuted by a juge d'instruction, of excessive stupidity, on the strength of the denunciation of a half-idiot girl, who accused the doctor of having performed an illegal operation upon her for thirty francs, would have been sent to penal servitude but for an explosion of public indignation, which had for result that he was immediately set at liberty by the Chief of the State. The honourable character given the condemned man by all his fellow-citizens made the grossness of the blunder self-evident. The magistrates themselves admitted it, and yet out of caste considerations they did all they could to prevent the pardon being signed. In all similar affairs the jury, confronted with technical details it is unable to understand, naturally hearkens to the public prosecutor, arguing that, after all, the affair has been investigated by magistrates trained to unravel the most intricate situations. Who, then, are the real authors of the error—the jurymen or the magistrates? We should cling vigorously to the jury. It constitutes, perhaps, the only category of crowd that cannot be replaced by any individuality. It alone can temper the severity of the law, which, equal for all, ought in principle to be blind and to take no cognisance of particular cases. Inaccessible to pity, and heeding nothing but the text of the law, the judge in his professional severity would visit with the same penalty the burglar guilty of murder and the wretched girl whom poverty and her abandonment by her seducer have driven to infanticide. The jury, on the other hand, instinctively feels that the seduced girl is much less guilty than the seducer, who, however, is not touched by the law, and that she deserves every indulgence.

Being well acquainted with the psychology of castes, and also with the psychology of other categories of crowds, I do not perceive a single case in which, wrongly accused of a crime, I should not prefer to have to deal with a jury rather than with magistrates. I should have some chance that my innocence would be recognised by the former and not the slightest chance that it would be admitted by the latter. The power of crowds is to be dreaded, but the power of certain castes is to be dreaded yet more. Crowds are open to conviction; castes never are.

CHAPTER IV: ELECTORAL CROWDS

General characteristics of electoral crowds—The manner of persuading them—The qualities that should be possessed by a candidate—Necessity of prestige—Why working men and peasants so rarely choose candidates from their own class—The influence of words and formulas on the elector—The general aspect of election oratory—How the opinions of the elector are formed—The power of political committees—They represent the most redoubtable form of tyranny—The committees of the Revolution— Universal suffrage cannot be replaced in spite of its slight psychological value—Why it is that the votes recorded would remain the same even if the right of voting were restricted to a limited class of citizens—What universal suffrage expresses in all countries.

ELECTORAL crowds—that is to say, collectivities invested with the power of electing the holders of certain functions—constitute heterogeneous crowds, but as their action is confined to a single clearly determined matter, namely, to choosing between different candidates, they present only a few of the characteristics previously described. Of the characteristics peculiar to crowds, they display in particular but slight aptitude for reasoning, the absence of the critical spirit, irritability, credulity, and simplicity. In their decision, moreover, is to be traced the influence of the leaders of crowds and the part played by the factors we have enumerated: affirmation, repetition, prestige, and contagion.

Let us examine by what methods electoral crowds are to be persuaded. It will be easy to deduce their psychology from the methods that are most successful.

It is of primary importance that the candidate should possess prestige. Personal prestige can only be replaced by that resulting from wealth. Talent and even genius are not elements of success of serious importance.

Of capital importance, on the other hand, is the necessity for the candidate of possessing prestige, of being able, that is, to force himself upon the electorate without discussion. The reason why the electors, of whom a majority are working men or peasants, so rarely choose a man from their own ranks to represent them is that such a person enjoys no prestige among them. When, by chance, they do elect a man who is their equal, it is as a rule for subsidiary reasons—for instance, to spite an eminent man, or an influential employer of labour on whom the elector is in daily dependence, and whose master he has the illusion he becomes in this way for a moment.

The possession of prestige does not suffice, however, to assure the success of a candidate. The elector stickles in particular for the flattery of his greed and vanity. He must be overwhelmed with the most extravagant blandishments, and there must be no hesitation in making him the most fantastic promises. If he is a working man it is impossible to go too far in insulting and stigmatising employers of labour. As for the rival candidate, an effort must be made to destroy his chance by establishing by dint of affirmation, repetition, and contagion that he is an arrant scoundrel, and that it is a matter of common knowledge that he has been guilty of several crimes. It is, of course, useless to trouble about any semblance of proof. Should the adversary be ill-acquainted with the psychology of crowds he will try to justify himself by arguments instead of confining himself to replying to one set of affirmations by another; and he will have no chance whatever of being successful.

The candidate's written programme should not be too categorical, since later on his adversaries might bring it up against him; in his verbal programme, however, there cannot be too much exaggeration. The most important reforms may be fearlessly promised. At the moment they are made these exaggerations produce a great effect, and they are not binding for the future, it being a matter of constant observation that the elector never troubles himself to know how far the candidate he has returned has followed out the electoral programme he applauded, and in virtue of which the election was supposed to have been secured.

In what precedes, all the factors of persuasion which we have described are to be recognised. We shall come across them again in the action exerted by words and formulas, whose magical sway we have already insisted upon. An orator who knows how to make use of these means of persuasion can do what he will with a crowd. Expressions such as infamous capital, vile exploiters, the admirable working man, the socialisation of wealth, &c., always produce the same effect, although already somewhat worn by use. But the candidate who hits on a new formula as devoid as possible of precise meaning, and apt in consequence to flatter the most varied aspirations, infallibly obtains a success. The sanguinary Spanish revolution of 1873 was brought about by one of these magical phrases of complex meaning on which everybody can put his own interpretation. A contemporary writer has described the launching of this phrase in terms that deserve to be quoted:—

"The radicals have made the discovery that a centralised republic is a monarchy in disguise, and to humour them the Cortes had unanimously proclaimed a FEDERAL REPUBLIC, though none of the voters could have explained what it was he had just voted for. This formula, however, delighted everybody; the joy was intoxicating, delirious. The reign of virtue and happiness had just been inaugurated on earth. A republican whose opponent refused him the title of federalist considered himself to be mortally insulted. People addressed each other in the streets with the words: `Long live the federal republic!' After which the praises were sung of the mystic virtue of the absence of discipline in the army, and of the autonomy of the soldiers. What was understood by the `federal republic?' There were those who took it to mean the emancipation of the provinces, institutions akin to those of the United States and administrative decentralisation; others had in view the abolition of all authority and the speedy commencement of the great social liquidation. The socialists of Barcelona and Andalusia stood out for the absolute sovereignty of the communes; they proposed to endow Spain with ten thousand independent municipalities, to legislate on their own account, and their creation to be accompanied by the suppression of the police and the army. In the southern provinces the insurrection was soon seen to spread from town to town and village to village. Directly a village had made its pronunciamento its first care was to destroy the telegraph wires and the railway lines so as to cut off all communication with its neighbours and Madrid. The sorriest hamlet was determined to stand on its own bottom. Federation had given place to cantonalism, marked by massacres, incendiarism, and every description of brutality, and bloody saturnalia were celebrated throughout the length and breadth of the land."

With respect to the influence that may be exerted by reasoning on the minds of electors, to harbour the least doubt on this subject can only be the result of never having read the reports of an electioneering meeting. In such a gathering affirmations, invectives, and sometimes blows are exchanged, but never arguments. Should silence be established for a moment it is because some one present, having the reputation of a "tough customer," has announced that he is about to heckle the candidate by putting him one of those embarrassing questions which are always the joy of the audience. The satisfaction, however, of the opposition party is shortlived, for the voice of the questioner is soon drowned in the uproar made by his adversaries. The following reports of public meetings, chosen from hundreds of similar examples, and taken from the daily papers, may be considered as typical:—

"One of the organisers of the meeting having asked the assembly to elect a president, the storm bursts. The anarchists leap on to the platform to take the committee table by storm. The socialists make an energetic defence; blows are exchanged, and each party accuses the other of being spies in the pay of the Government, &c.... A citizen leaves the hall with a black eye.

"The committee is at length installed as best it may be in the midst of the tumult, and the right to speak devolves upon `Comrade' X.

"The orator starts a vigorous attack on the socialists, who interrupt him with shouts of `Idiot, scoundrel, blackguard!' &c., epithets to which Comrade X. replies by setting forth a theory according to which the socialists are `idiots' or `jokers.'"

"The Allemanist party had organised yesterday evening, in the Hall of Commerce, in the Rue du Faubourg-du-Temple, a great meeting, preliminary to the workers' fete of the 1st of May. The watchword of the meeting was `Calm and Tranquillity!'

"Comrade G—— alludes to the socialists as `idiots' and `humbugs.'

"At these words there is an exchange of invectives and orators and audience come to blows. Chairs, tables, and benches are converted into weapons," &c., &c.

It is not to be imagined for a moment that this description of discussion is peculiar to a determined class of electors and dependent on their social position. In every anonymous assembly whatever, though it be composed exclusively of highly educated persons, discussion always assumes the same shape. I have shown that when men are collected in a crowd there is a tendency towards their mental levelling at work, and proof of this is to be found at every turn. Take, for example, the following extract from a report of a meeting composed exclusively of students, which I borrow from the Temps of 13th of February, 1895:—

"The tumult only increased as the evening went on; I do not believe that a single orator succeeded in uttering two sentences without being interrupted. At every instant there came shouts from this or that direction or from every direction at once. Applause was intermingled with hissing, violent discussions were in progress between individual members of the audience, sticks were brandished threateningly, others beat a tattoo on the floor, and the interrupters were greeted with yells of `Put him out!' or `Let him speak!'

"M. C—— lavished such epithets as odious and cowardly, monstrous, vile, venal and vindictive, on the Association, which he declared he wanted to destroy," &c., &c.

How, it may be asked, can an elector form an opinion under such conditions? To put such a question is to harbour a strange delusion as to the measure of liberty that may be enjoyed by a collectivity. Crowds have opinions that have been imposed upon them, but they never boast reasoned opinions. In the case under consideration the opinions and votes of the electors are in the hands of the election committees, whose leading spirits are, as a rule, publicans, their influence over the working men, to whom they allow credit, being great. "Do you know what an election committee is?" writes M. Scherer, one of the most valiant champions of present-day democracy. "It is neither more nor less than the corner-stone of our institutions, the masterpiece of the political machine. France is governed to-day by the election committees."

To exert an influence over them is not difficult, provided the candidate be in himself acceptable and possess adequate financial resources. According to the admissions of the donors, three millions of francs sufficed to secure the repeated elections of General Boulanger.

Such is the psychology of electoral crowds. It is identical with that of other crowds: neither better nor worse.

In consequence I draw no conclusion against universal suffrage from what precedes. Had I to settle its fate, I should preserve it as it is for practical reasons, which are to be deduced in point of fact from our investigation of the psychology of crowds. On this account I shall proceed to set them forth.

No doubt the weak side of universal suffrage is too obvious to be overlooked. It cannot be gainsaid that civilisation has been the work of a small minority of superior intelligences constituting the culminating point of a pyramid, whose stages, widening in proportion to the decrease of mental power, represent the masses of a nation. The greatness of a civilisation cannot assuredly depend upon the votes given by inferior elements boasting solely numerical strength. Doubtless, too, the votes recorded by crowds are often very dangerous. They have already cost us several invasions, and in view of the triumph of socialism, for which they are preparing the way, it is probable that the vagaries of popular sovereignty will cost us still more dearly.

Excellent, however, as these objections are in theory, in practice they lose all force, as will be admitted if the invincible strength be remembered of ideas transformed into dogmas. The dogma of the sovereignty of crowds is as little defensible, from the philosophical point of view, as the religious dogmas of the Middle Ages, but it enjoys at present the same absolute power they formerly enjoyed. It is as unattackable in consequence as in the past were our religious ideas. Imagine a modern freethinker miraculously transported into the midst of the Middle Ages. Do you suppose that, after having ascertained the sovereign power of the religious ideas that were then in force, he would have been tempted to attack them? Having fallen into the hands of a judge disposed to send him to the stake, under the imputation of having concluded a pact with the devil, or of having been present at the witches sabbath, would it have occurred to him to call in question the existence of the devil or of the sabbath? It were as wise to oppose cyclones with discussion as the beliefs of crowds. The dogma of universal suffrage possesses to-day the power the Christian dogmas formerly possessed. Orators and writers allude to it with a respect and adulation that never fell to the share of Louis XIV. In consequence the same position must be taken up with regard to it as with regard to all religious dogmas. Time alone can act upon them.

Besides, it would be the more useless to attempt to undermine this dogma, inasmuch as it has an appearance of reasonableness in its favour. "In an era of equality," Tocqueville justly remarks, "men have no faith in each other on account of their being all alike; yet this same similitude gives them an almost limitless confidence in the judgment of the public, the reason being that it does not appear probable that, all men being equally enlightened, truth and numerical superiority should not go hand in hand."

Must it be believed that with a restricted suffrage—a suffrage restricted to those intellectually capable if it be desired—an improvement would be effected in the votes of crowds? I cannot admit for a moment that this would be the case, and that for the reasons I have already given touching the mental inferiority of all collectivities, whatever their composition. In a crowd men always tend to the same level, and, on general questions, a vote, recorded by forty academicians is no better than that of forty water-carriers. I do not in the least believe that any of the votes for which universal suffrage is blamed—the re-establishment of the Empire, for instance— would have fallen out differently had the voters been exclusively recruited among learned and liberally educated men. It does not follow because an individual knows Greek or mathematics, is an architect, a veterinary surgeon, a doctor, or a barrister, that he is endowed with a special intelligence of social questions. All our political economists are highly educated, being for the most part professors or academicians, yet is there a single general question—protection, bimetallism, &c.—on which they have succeeded in agreeing? The explanation is that their science is only a very attenuated form of our universal ignorance. With regard to social problems, owing to the number of unknown quantities they offer, men are substantially, equally ignorant.

In consequence, were the electorate solely composed of persons stuffed with sciences their votes would be no better than those emitted at present. They would be guided in the main by their sentiments and by party spirit. We should be spared none of the difficulties we now have to contend with, and we should certainly be subjected to the oppressive tyranny of castes.

Whether the suffrage of crowds be restricted or general, whether it be exercised under a republic or a monarchy, in

France, in Belgium, in Greece, in Portugal, or in Spain, it is everywhere identical; and, when all is said and done, it is the expression of the unconscious aspirations and needs of the race. In each country the average opinions of those elected represent the genius of the race, and they will be found not to alter sensibly from one generation to another.

It is seen, then, that we are confronted once more by the fundamental notion of race, which we have come across so often, and on this other notion, which is the outcome of the first, that institutions and governments play but a small part in the life of a people. Peoples are guided in the main by the genius of their race, that is, by that inherited residue of qualities of which the genius is the sum total. Race and the slavery of our daily necessities are the mysterious master-causes that rule our destiny.

CHAPTER V: PARLIAMENTARY ASSEMBLIES

Parliamentary crowds present most of the characteristics common to heterogeneous crowds that are not anonymous—The simplicity of their opinions—Their suggestibility and its limits—Their indestructible, fixed opinions and their changed opinions—The reason of the predominance of indecision—The role of the leaders—The reason of their prestige—They are the true masters of an assembly whose votes, on that account, are merely those of a small minority—The absolute power they exercise—The elements of their oratorical art—Phrases and images—The psychological necessity the leaders are under of being in a general way of stubborn convictions and narrow-minded—It is impossible for a speaker without prestige to obtain recognition for his arguments— The exaggeration of the sentiments, whether good or bad, of assemblies— At certain moments they become automatic—The sittings of the Convention—Cases in which an assembly loses the characteristics of crowds—The influence of specialists when technical questions arise—The advantages and dangers of a parliamentary system in all countries—It is adapted to modern needs; but it involves financial waste and the progressive curtailment of all liberty—Conclusion.

In parliamentary assemblies we have an example of heterogeneous crowds that are not anonymous. Although the mode of election of their members varies from epoch to epoch, and from nation to nation, they present very similar characteristics. In this case the influence of the race makes itself felt to weaken or exaggerate the characteristics common to crowds, but not to prevent their manifestation. The parliamentary assemblies of the most widely different countries, of Greece, Italy, Portugal, Spain, France, and America present great analogies in their debates and votes, and leave the respective governments face to face with identical difficulties.

Moreover, the parliamentary system represents the ideal of all modern civilised peoples. The system is the expression of the idea, psychologically erroneous, but generally admitted, that a large gathering of men is much more capable than a small number of coming to a wise and independent decision on a given subject.

The general characteristics of crowds are to be met with in parliamentary assemblies: intellectual simplicity, irritability, suggestibility, the exaggeration of the sentiments and the preponderating influence of a few leaders. In consequence, however, of their special composition parliamentary crowds offer some distinctive features, which we shall point out shortly.

Simplicity in their opinions is one of their most important characteristics. In the case of all parties, and more especially so far as the Latin peoples are concerned, an invariable tendency is met with in crowds of this kind to solve the most complicated social problems by the simplest abstract principles and general laws applicable to all cases. Naturally the principles vary with the party; but owing to the mere fact that the individual members are a part of a crowd, they are always inclined to exaggerate the worth of their principles, and to push them to their extreme consequences. In consequence parliaments are more especially representative of extreme opinions.

The most perfect example of the ingenuous simplification of opinions peculiar to assemblies is offered by the Jacobins of the French Revolution. Dogmatic and logical to a man, and their brains full of vague generalities, they busied themselves with the application of fixed-principles without concerning themselves with events. It has been said of them, with reason, that they went through the Revolution without witnessing it. With the aid of the very simple dogmas that served them as guide, they imagined they could recast society from top to bottom, and cause a highly refined civilisation to return to a very anterior phase of the social evolution. The methods they resorted to to realise their dream wore the same stamp of absolute ingenuousness. They confined themselves, in reality, to destroying what stood in their way. All of them, moreover—Girondists, the Men of the Mountain, the Thermidorians, &c.—were alike animated by the same spirit.

Parliamentary crowds are very open to suggestion; and, as in the case of all crowds, the suggestion comes from leaders possessing prestige; but the suggestibility of parliamentary assemblies has very clearly defined limits, which it is important to point out.

On all questions of local or regional interest every member of an assembly has fixed, unalterable opinions, which no amount of argument can shake. The talent of a Demosthenes would be powerless to change the vote of a Deputy on such questions as protection or the privilege of distilling alcohol, questions in which the interests of influential electors are involved. The suggestion emanating from these electors and undergone before the time to vote arrives, sufficiently outweighs suggestions from any other source to annul them and to maintain an absolute fixity of opinion.

On general questions—the overthrow of a Cabinet, the imposition of a tax, &c.—there is no longer any fixity of opinion, and the suggestions of leaders can exert an influence, though not in quite the same way as in an ordinary crowd. Every party has its leaders, who possess occasionally an equal influence. The result is that the Deputy finds himself placed between two contrary suggestions, and is inevitably made to hesitate. This explains how it is that he is often seen to vote in contrary fashion in an interval of a quarter of an hour or to add to a law an article which nullifies it; for instance, to withdraw from employers of labour the right of choosing and dismissing their workmen, and then to very nearly annul this measure by an amendment.

It is for the same reason that every Chamber that is returned has some very stable opinions, and other opinions that are very shifting. On the whole, the general questions being the more numerous, indecision is predominant in the Chamber—the indecision which results from the ever- present fear of the elector, the suggestion received from whom is always latent, and tends to counterbalance the influence of the leaders.

Still, it is the leaders who are definitely the masters in those numerous discussions, with regard to the subject-matter of which the members of an assembly are without strong preconceived opinions.

The necessity for these leaders is evident, since, under the name of heads of groups, they are met with in the assemblies of every country. They are the real rulers of an assembly. Men forming a crowd cannot do without a master, whence it results that the votes of an assembly only represent, as a rule, the opinions of a small minority.

The influence of the leaders is due in very small measure to the arguments they employ, but in a large degree to their prestige. The best proof of this is that, should they by any circumstance lose their prestige, their influence disappears.

The prestige of these political leaders is individual, and independent of name or celebrity: a fact of which M. Jules Simon gives us some very curious examples in his remarks on the prominent men of the Assembly of 1848, of which he was a member:—

"Two months before he was all-powerful, Louis Napoleon was entirely without the least importance.

"Victor Hugo mounted the tribune. He failed to achieve success. He was listened to as Felix Pyat was listened to, but he did not obtain as much applause. `I don't like his ideas,' Vaulabelle said to me, speaking of Felix Pyat,' but he is one of the greatest writers and the greatest orator of France.' Edgar Quinet, in spite of his exceptional and powerful intelligence, was held in no esteem whatever. He had been popular for awhile before the opening of the Assembly; in the Assembly he had no popularity.

"The splendour of genius makes itself less felt in political assemblies than anywhere else. They only give heed to eloquence appropriate to the time and place and to party services, not to services rendered the country. For homage to be rendered Lamartine in 1848 and Thiers in 1871, the stimulant was needed of urgent, inexorable interest. As soon as the danger was passed the parliamentary world forgot in the same instant its gratitude and its fright."

I have quoted the preceding passage for the sake of the facts it contains, not of the explanations it offers, their psychology being somewhat poor. A crowd would at once lose its character of a crowd were it to credit its leaders with their services, whether of a party nature or rendered their country. The crowd that obeys a leader is under the influence of his prestige, and its submission is not dictated by any sentiment of interest or gratitude.

In consequence the leader endowed with sufficient prestige wields almost absolute power. The immense influence exerted during a long series of years, thanks to his prestige, by a celebrated Deputy, beaten at the last general election in consequence of certain financial events, is well known. He had only to give the signal and Cabinets were overthrown. A writer has clearly indicated the scope of his action in the following lines:—

"It is due, in the main, to M. X—— that we paid three times as dearly as we should have done for Tonkin, that we remained so long on a precarious footing in Madagascar, that we were defrauded of an empire in the region of the Lower Niger, and that we have lost the preponderating situation we used to occupy in Egypt. The theories of M. X—— have cost us more territories than the disasters of Napoleon I."

We must not harbour too bitter a grudge against the leader in question. It is plain that he has cost us very dear; but a great part of his influence was due to the fact that he followed public opinion, which, in colonial matters, was far from being at the time what it has since become. A leader is seldom in advance of public opinion; almost always all he does is to follow it and to espouse all its errors.

The means of persuasion of the leaders we are dealing with, apart from their prestige, consist in the factors we have already enumerated several times. To make a skilful use of these resources a leader must have arrived at a comprehension, at least in an unconscious manner, of the psychology of crowds, and must know how to address them. He should be aware, in particular, of the fascinating influence of words, phrases, and images. He should possess a special description of eloquence, composed of energetic affirmations—unburdened with proofs— and impressive images, accompanied by very summary arguments. This is a kind of eloquence that is met with in all assemblies, the

English Parliament included, the most serious though it is of all.

"Debates in the House of Commons," says the English philosopher Maine, "may be constantly read in which the entire discussion is confined to an exchange of rather weak generalities and rather violent personalities. General formulas of this description exercise a prodigious influence on the imagination of a pure democracy. It will always be easy to make a crowd accept general assertions, presented in striking terms, although they have never been verified, and are perhaps not susceptible of verification."

Too much importance cannot be attached to the "striking terms" alluded to in the above quotation. We have already insisted, on several occasions, on the special power of words and formulas. They must be chosen in such a way as to evoke very vivid images. The following phrase, taken from a speech by one of the leaders of our assemblies, affords an excellent example:—

"When the same vessel shall bear away to the fever-haunted lands of our penitentiary settlements the politician of shady reputation and the anarchist guilty of murder, the pair will be able to converse together, and they will appear to each other as the two complementary aspects of one and the same state of society."

The image thus evoked is very vivid, and all the adversaries of the speaker felt themselves threatened by it. They conjured up a double vision of the fever-haunted country and the vessel that may carry them away; for is it not possible that they are included in the somewhat ill-defined category of the politicians menaced? They experienced the lurking fear that the men of the Convention must have felt whom the vague speeches of Robespierre threatened with the guillotine, and who, under the influence of this fear, invariably yielded to him.

It is all to the interest of the leaders to indulge in the most improbable exaggerations. The speaker of whom I have just cited a sentence was able to affirm, without arousing violent protestations, that bankers and priests had subsidised the throwers of bombs, and that the directors of the great financial companies deserve the same punishment as anarchists. Affirmations of this kind are always effective with crowds. The affirmation is never too violent, the declamation never too threatening. Nothing intimidates the audience more than this sort of eloquence. Those present are afraid that if they protest they will be put down as traitors or accomplices.

As I have said, this peculiar style of eloquence has ever been of sovereign effect in all assemblies. In times of crisis its power is still further accentuated. The speeches of the great orators of the assemblies of the French Revolution are very interesting reading from this point of view. At every instant they thought themselves obliged to pause in order to denounce crime and exalt virtue, after which they would burst forth into imprecations against tyrants, and swear to live free men or perish. Those present rose to their feet, applauded furiously, and then, calmed, took their seats again.

On occasion, the leader may be intelligent and highly educated, but the possession of these qualities does him, as a rule, more harm than good. By showing how complex things are, by allowing of explanation and promoting comprehension, intelligence always renders its owner indulgent, and blunts, in a large measure, that intensity and violence of conviction needful for apostles. The great leaders of crowds of all ages, and those of the Revolution in particular, have been of lamentably narrow intellect; while it is precisely those whose intelligence has been the most restricted who have exercised the greatest influence.

The speeches of the most celebrated of them, of Robespierre, frequently astound one by their incoherence: by merely reading them no plausible explanation is to be found of the great part played by the powerful dictator:—

"The commonplaces and redundancies of pedagogic eloquence and Latin culture at the service of a mind childish rather than undistinguished, and limited in its notions of attack and defence to the defiant attitude of schoolboys. Not an idea, not a happy turn of phrase, or a telling hit: a storm of declamation that leaves us bored. After a dose of this unexhilarating reading one is attempted to exclaim `Oh!' with the amiable Camille Desmoulins."

It is terrible at times to think of the power that strong conviction combined with extreme narrowness of mind gives a man possessing prestige. It is none the less necessary that these conditions should be satisfied for a man to ignore obstacles and display strength of will in a high measure. Crowds instinctively recognise in men of energy and conviction the masters they are always in need of.

In a parliamentary assembly the success of a speech depends almost solely on the prestige possessed by the speaker, and not at all on the arguments he brings forward. The best proof of this is that when for one cause or another a speaker loses his prestige, he loses simultaneously all his influence, that is, his power of influencing votes at will.

When an unknown speaker comes forward with a speech containing good arguments, but only arguments, the chances are that he will only obtain a hearing. A Deputy who is a psychologist of insight, M. Desaubes, has recently traced in the following lines the portrait of the Deputy who lacks prestige:—

"When he takes his place in the tribune he draws a document from his portfolio, spreads it out methodically before him, and makes a start with assurance.

"He flatters himself that he will implant in the minds of his audience the conviction by which he is himself animated. He has weighed and reweighed his arguments; he is well primed with figures and proofs; he is certain he will convince his hearers. In the face of the evidence he is to adduce all resistance would be futile. He begins, confident in the justice of his cause, and relying upon the attention of his colleagues, whose only anxiety, of course, is to subscribe to the truth.

"He speaks, and is at once surprised at the restlessness of the

House, and a little annoyed by the noise that is being made.

"How is it silence is not kept? Why this general inattention? What are those Deputies thinking about who are engaged in conversation? What urgent motive has induced this or that Deputy to quit his seat?

"An expression of uneasiness crosses his face; he frowns and stops. Encouraged by the President, he begins again, raising his voice. He is only listened to all the less. He lends emphasis to his words, and gesticulates: the noise around him increases. He can no longer hear himself, and again stops; finally, afraid that his silence may provoke the dreaded cry, `The Closure!' he starts off again. The clamour becomes unbearable."

When parliamentary assemblies reach a certain pitch of excitement they become identical with ordinary heterogeneous crowds, and their sentiments in consequence present the peculiarity of being always extreme. They will be seen to commit acts of the greatest heroism or the worst excesses. The individual is no longer himself, and so entirely is this the case that he will vote measures most adverse to his personal interests.

The history of the French Revolution shows to what an extent assemblies are capable of losing their self-consciousness, and of obeying suggestions most contrary to their interests. It was an enormous sacrifice for the nobility to renounce its privileges, yet it did so without hesitation on a famous night during the sittings of the Constituant Assembly. By renouncing their inviolability the men of the Convention placed themselves under a perpetual menace of death and yet they took this step, and were not afraid to decimate their own ranks, though perfectly aware that the scaffold to which they were sending their colleagues to-day might be their own fate to-morrow. The truth is they had attained to that completely automatic state which I have described elsewhere, and no consideration would hinder them from yielding to the suggestions by which they were hypnotised. The following passage from the memoirs of one of them, Billaud-Varennes, is absolutely typical on this score: "The decisions with which we have been so reproached," he says, "WERE NOT DESIRED BY US TWO DAYS, A SINGLE DAY BEFORE THEY WERE TAKEN: IT WAS THE CRISIS AND NOTHING ELSE THAT GAVE RISE TO THEM." Nothing can be more accurate.

The same phenomena of unconsciousness were to be witnessed during all the stormy sittings of the Convention.

"They approved and decreed measures," says Taine, "which they held in horror—measures which were not only stupid and foolish, but measures that were crimes—the murder of innocent men, the murder of their friends. The Left, supported by the Right, unanimously and amid loud applause, sent to the scaffold Danton, its natural chief, and the great promoter and leader of the Revolution. Unanimously and amid the greatest applause the Right, supported by the Left, votes the worst decrees of the revolutionary government. Unanimously and amid cries of admiration and enthusiasm, amid demonstrations of passionate sympathy for Collot d'Herbois, Couthon, and Robespierre, the Convention by spontaneous and repeated re-elections keeps in office the homicidal government which the Plain detests because it is homicidal, and the Mountain detests because it is decimated by it. The Plain and the Mountain, the majority and the minority, finish by consenting to help on their own suicide. The 22 Prairial the entire Convention offered itself to the executioner; the 8 Thermidor, during the first quarter of an hour that followed Robespierre's speech, it did the same thing again."

This picture may appear sombre. Yet it is accurate. Parliamentary assemblies, sufficiently excited and hypnotised, offer the same characteristics. They become an unstable flock, obedient to every impulsion. The following description of the Assembly of 1848 is due to M. Spuller, a parliamentarian whose faith in democracy is above suspicion. I reproduce it from the Revue litteraire, and it is thoroughly typical. It offers an example of all the exaggerated sentiments which I have described as characteristic of crowds, and of that excessive changeableness which permits of assemblies passing, from moment to moment, from one set of sentiments to another entirely opposite.

"The Republican party was brought to its perdition by its divisions, its jealousies, its suspicions, and, in turn, its blind confidence and its limitless hopes. Its ingenuousness and candour were only equalled by its universal mistrust. An absence of all sense of legality, of all comprehension of discipline, together with boundless terrors and illusions; the peasant and the child are on a level in these respects. Their calm is as great as their impatience; their ferocity is equal to their docility. This condition is the natural consequence of a temperament that is not formed and of the lack of education. Nothing astonishes such persons, and everything disconcerts them. Trembling with fear or brave to the point of heroism, they would go through fire and water or fly from a shadow.

"They are ignorant of cause and effect and of the connecting links between events. They are as promptly discouraged as they are exalted, they are subject to every description of panic, they are always either too highly strung or too downcast, but never in the mood or the measure the situation would require. More fluid than water they reflect every line and assume every shape. What sort of a foundation for a government can they be expected to supply?"

Fortunately all the characteristics just described as to be met with in parliamentary assemblies are in no wise constantly displayed. Such assemblies only constitute crowds at certain moments. The individuals composing them retain their individuality in a great number of cases, which explains how it is that an assembly is able to turn out excellent technical laws. It is true that the author of these laws is a specialist who has prepared them in the quiet of his study, and that in reality the law voted is the work of an individual and not of an assembly. These laws are naturally the best. They are only liable to have disastrous results when a series of amendments has converted them into the outcome of a collective effort. The work of a crowd is always inferior, whatever its nature, to that of an isolated individual. It is specialists who safeguard assemblies from passing ill-advised or unworkable measures. The specialist in this case is a temporary leader of crowds. The Assembly is without influence on him, but he has influence over the Assembly.

In spite of all the difficulties attending their working, parliamentary assemblies are the best form of government mankind has discovered as yet, and more especially the best means it has found to escape the yoke of personal tyrannies. They constitute assuredly the ideal government at any rate for philosophers, thinkers, writers, artists, and learned men—in a word, for all those who form the cream of a civilisation.

Moreover, in reality they only present two serious dangers, one being inevitable financial waste, and the other the progressive restriction of the liberty of the individual.

The first of these dangers is the necessary consequence of the exigencies and want of foresight of electoral crowds. Should a member of an assembly propose a measure giving apparent satisfaction to democratic ideas, should he bring in a Bill, for instance, to assure old-age pensions to all workers, and to increase the wages of any class of State employes, the other Deputies, victims of suggestion in their dread of their electors, will not venture to seem to disregard the interests of the latter by rejecting the proposed measure, although well aware they are imposing a fresh strain on the Budget and necessitating the creation of new taxes. It is impossible for them to hesitate to give their votes. The consequences of the increase of expenditure are remote and will not entail disagreeable consequences for them personally, while the consequences of a negative vote might clearly come to light when they next present themselves for re-election.

In addition to this first cause of an exaggerated expenditure there is another not less imperative—the necessity of voting all grants for local purposes. A Deputy is unable to oppose grants of this kind because they represent once more the exigencies of the electors, and because each individual Deputy can only obtain what he requires for his own constituency on the condition of acceding to similar demands on the part of his colleagues.

The second of the dangers referred to above—the inevitable restrictions on liberty consummated by parliamentary assemblies—is apparently less obvious, but is, nevertheless, very real. It is the result of the innumerable laws—having always a restrictive action—which parliaments consider themselves obliged to vote and to whose consequences, owing to their shortsightedness, they are in a great measure blind.

The danger must indeed be most inevitable, since even England itself, which assuredly offers the most popular type of the parliamentary regime, the type in which the representative is most independent of his elector, has been unable to escape it. Herbert Spencer has shown, in a work already old, that the increase of apparent liberty must needs be followed by the decrease of real liberty. Returning to this contention in his recent book, "The Individual versus the State," he thus expresses himself with regard to the English Parliament:—

"Legislation since this period has followed the course, I pointed out. Rapidly multiplying dictatorial measures have continually tended to restrict individual liberties, and this in two ways. Regulations have been established every year in greater number, imposing a constraint on the citizen in matters in which his acts were formerly completely free, and forcing him to accomplish acts which he was formerly at liberty to accomplish or not to accomplish at will. At the same time heavier and heavier public, and especially local, burdens have still further restricted his liberty by diminishing the portion of his profits he can spend as he chooses, and by augmenting the portion which is taken from him to be spent according to the good pleasure of the public authorities."

This progressive restriction of liberties shows itself in every country in a special shape which Herbert Spencer has not pointed out; it is that the passing of these innumerable series of legislative measures, all of them in a general way of a restrictive order, conduces necessarily to augment the number, the power, and the influence of the functionaries charged with their application. These functionaries tend in this way to become the veritable masters of civilised countries. Their power is all the greater owing to the fact that, amidst the incessant transfer of authority, the administrative caste is alone in being untouched by these changes, is alone in possessing irresponsibility, impersonality, and perpetuity. There is no more oppressive despotism than that which presents itself under this triple form.

This incessant creation of restrictive laws and regulations, surrounding the pettiest actions of existence with the most complicated formalities, inevitably has for its result the confining within narrower and narrower limits of the sphere in which the citizen may move freely. Victims of the delusion that equality and liberty are the better assured by the multiplication of laws, nations daily consent to put up with trammels increasingly burdensome. They do not accept this legislation with impunity. Accustomed to put up with every yoke, they soon end by desiring servitude, and lose all spontaneousness and energy. They are then no more than vain shadows, passive, unresisting and powerless automata.

Arrived at this point, the individual is bound to seek outside himself the forces he no longer finds within him. The functions of governments necessarily increase in proportion as the indifference and helplessness of the citizens grow. They it is who must necessarily exhibit the initiative, enterprising, and guiding spirit in which private persons are lacking. It falls on them to undertake everything, direct everything, and take everything under their protection. The State becomes an all-powerful god. Still experience shows that the power of such gods was never either very durable or very strong.

This progressive restriction of all liberties in the case of certain peoples, in spite of an outward license that gives them the illusion that these liberties are still in their possession, seems at least as much a consequence of their old age as of any particular system. It constitutes one of the precursory symptoms of that decadent phase which up to now no civilisation has escaped.

Judging by the lessons of the past, and by the symptoms that strike the attention on every side, several of our modern civilisations have reached that phase of extreme old age which precedes decadence. It seems inevitable that all peoples should pass through identical phases of existence, since history is so often seen to repeat its course.

It is easy to note briefly these common phases of the evolution of civilisations, and I shall terminate this work with a summary of them. This rapid sketch will perhaps throw some gleams of light on the causes of the power at present wielded by crowds.

If we examine in their main lines the genesis of the greatness and of the fall of the civilisations that preceded our own, what do we see?

At the dawn of civilisation a swarm of men of various origin, brought together by the chances of migrations, invasions, and conquests. Of different blood, and of equally different languages and beliefs, the only common bond of union between these men is the half-recognised law of a chief. The psychological characteristics of crowds are present in an eminent degree in these confused agglomerations. They have the transient cohesion of crowds, their heroism, their weaknesses, their impulsiveness, and their violence. Nothing is stable in connection with them. They are barbarians.

At length time accomplishes its work. The identity of surroundings, the repeated intermingling of races, the necessities of life in common exert their influence. The assemblage of dissimilar units begins to blend into a whole, to form a race; that is, an aggregate possessing common characteristics and sentiments to which heredity will give greater and greater fixity. The crowd has become a people, and this people is able to emerge from its barbarous state. However, it will only entirely emerge therefrom when, after long efforts, struggles necessarily repeated, and innumerable recommencements, it shall have acquired an ideal. The nature of this ideal is of slight importance; whether it be the cult of Rome, the might of Athens, or the triumph of Allah, it will suffice to endow all the individuals of the race that is forming with perfect unity of sentiment and thought.

At this stage a new civilisation, with its institutions, its beliefs, and its arts, may be born. In pursuit of its ideal, the race will acquire in succession the qualities necessary to give it splendour, vigour, and grandeur. At times no doubt it will still be a crowd, but henceforth, beneath the mobile and changing characteristics of crowds, is found a solid substratum, the genius of the race which confines within narrow limits the transformations of a nation and overrules the play of chance.

After having exerted its creative action, time begins that work of destruction from which neither gods nor men escape. Having reached a certain level of strength and complexity a civilisation ceases to grow, and having ceased to grow it is condemned to a speedy decline. The hour of its old age has struck.

This inevitable hour is always marked by the weakening of the ideal that was the mainstay of the race. In proportion as this ideal pales all the religious, political, and social structures inspired by it begin to be shaken.

With the progressive perishing of its ideal the race loses more and more the qualities that lent it its cohesion, its unity, and its strength. The personality and intelligence of the individual may increase, but at the same time this collective egoism of the race is replaced by an excessive development of the egoism of the individual, accompanied by a weakening of character and a lessening of the capacity for action. What constituted a people, a unity, a whole, becomes in the end an agglomeration of individualities lacking cohesion, and artificially held together for a time by its traditions and institutions. It is at this stage that men, divided by their interests and aspirations, and incapable any longer of self-government, require directing in their pettiest acts, and that the State exerts an absorbing influence.

With the definite loss of its old ideal the genius of the race entirely disappears; it is a mere swarm of isolated individuals and returns to its original state—that of a crowd. Without consistency and without a future, it has all the transitory characteristics of crowds. Its civilisation is now without stability, and at the mercy of every chance. The populace is sovereign, and the tide of barbarism mounts. The civilisation may still seem brilliant because it possesses an outward front, the work of a long past, but it is in reality an edifice crumbling to ruin, which nothing supports, and destined to fall in at the first storm.

To pass in pursuit of an ideal from the barbarous to the civilised state, and then, when this ideal has lost its virtue, to decline and die, such is the cycle of the life of a people.

Printed in Great Britain
by Amazon

27842617R00034